Weaving Evidence, Inquiry and Standards to Build Better Schools

Editors: Helen Timperley and Judy Parr

NZCER PRESS

Wellington 2010

NZCER PRESS

New Zealand Council for Educational Research
PO Box 3237
Wellington
New Zealand

© Helen Timperley and Judy Parr, 2010

ISBN 978-1-877398-60-5

Designed by Cluster Creative

Printed by Printlink, Wellington

Distributed by NZCER Distribution Services
PO Box 3237
Wellington
New Zealand
www.nzcer.org.nz

Contents

Preface

Every school leader and teacher knows that the challenges of change are constant and ongoing. What was accepted in previous years is no longer sufficient. Expectations have risen, particularly as New Zealand has sought to raise the achievement of all its students, with a major focus on the underachievement of some groups across the nation's schools.

The material for this book has arisen from our involvement in different research and development projects that were designed to improve students' learning and achievement. Major contributions have been made to this work by teachers and leaders working in schools, and by members of the professional development community. The results have been promising. Late in 2007 we came together as a team in a research and development project designed to build evaluative capability in schooling improvement across clusters of schools in New Zealand.

Following an initial year of research, evaluation and development we decided that we could be more helpful to schools if we made the thinking behind the issues we raised and the suggestions we offered more explicit. As a result, we paused in our research and evaluation activities to write a series of position papers on various aspects of schooling improvement. Draft papers were shared in cross-sector meetings with a large number of school leaders, teachers and professional developers.

Feedback on the usefulness of the position papers from these people engaged in building better schools was very positive, but they wanted more: more explanation, more case examples and more descriptions of how to make faster progress. These requests for more demonstrated their high level of commitment to building better schools. This book is our response. The original papers have been rewritten and case examples reworked to make them more relevant to individual schools that are looking for direction in building better schools.

This is not a "how to" book with all the answers. It is a book designed to provoke thinking and talking by those engaging in improvement activities, and to provide sets of principles and suggestions for processes that need to be considered in any development efforts.

As with any book, the ideas have been influenced by those with whom we work and those whose books and papers we read. It would be impossible to acknowledge them all because much of the thinking has developed over many years through iterative cycles of research and development. However, we do wish to acknowledge all those professional developers, school leaders and teachers who have challenged our thinking, demanded we offer something useful and told us when something does not work (and when it does). Without their input our ideas would not have stood the tests of reality.

A special acknowledgement must go to the Ministry of Education. Much of the research in which we have engaged has been supported with funding from the Ministry. More importantly, a number of people within the Ministry have engaged with our ideas and challenged our thinking. These people have acted in ways consistent with the best sense of being public servants. They have rolled up their sleeves and demonstrated their commitment to raising achievement and reducing disparities in very real ways in New Zealand schools. At the same time we must acknowledge that the material presented in this book represents the ideas of the authors and does not necessarily represent either the policy or practice of the Ministry of Education. Copyright in the position papers is held by the Crown and the Ministry has agreed to our use of that material in this book.

We are also grateful for the involvement and critique of many schools from the Building Evaluative Capability in Schooling Improvement Project in particular, but also schools from our wider research activities. Although the book is written for schools, it could not have been written without their involvement.

ONE

THE BIG PICTURE

1

Evidence, Inquiry and Standards

Helen Timperley and Judy Parr

Every day, school leaders and teachers face the challenges of introducing new curricula, assessment approaches and technologies to a changing student population. It has now become a truism that yesterday's knowledge and instructional practices are insufficient to meet the information and knowledge needs of students today. As Ben Levin (2008) says, "The world changes, so must schools" (p. 2).

There are many different ways to meet the challenge of changing to build better schools. This book is based on the premise that the approach most likely to promote student learning is for leaders and teachers to:

- use a range of evidence to inquire into the effectiveness of current practices
- decide what should stay because it is working
- decide what needs to change, and how it needs to change.

Professional learning opportunities for leaders and teachers are then designed to address the changes, and the effectiveness of everyone's efforts is checked and new challenges are identified. The processes involved are not as simple as this description makes them appear, however, and this book unpacks the ideas underpinning them.

The New Zealand Curriculum and Te Marautanga o Aotearoa (Ministry of Education,

2007a, 2007b) and the themes of this book share a common thrust. The curriculum documents emphasise teaching as a process of inquiry, and this book focuses on the skills to both inquire into and evaluate practice for its impact on students, and then work out how to address any discrepancies. However, that shared emphasis on inquiry itself brings challenges as schools work out how to tailor the contents of the Curriculum to best fit their own context. This tailoring requires detailed evidence of the needs of the students in particular school contexts, and evidence of the quality of teaching to address those needs within the broad constraints of the Curriculum for each area.

Schools must also work to integrate the idea of key competencies—the higher order goals of learning for students—into their teaching and learning programmes. Students must be given the opportunity to become proficient in these competencies through learning experiences across all curriculum areas. Planning so that this happens systematically, and deciding how to evaluate the effectiveness of the implementation of both the Curriculum and key competencies, requires considerable knowledge and skill—together with evidence of effectiveness.

Another challenge comes from the shift in our understanding of the purpose of assessment. The idea that assessments are a source of evidence for sorting, labelling and credentialling students has changed. Both internationally and in New Zealand, researchers have found that those teachers and school leaders who use assessment information to find out what it is students know and can do in relation to the Curriculum, and use this information to identify what needs to be taught next, usually show gains in student achievement beyond those expected (e.g., Elmore, 2004; Lai, McNaughton, Timperley, & Hsiao, 2009; Timperley & Parr, 2009; Wiliam, 2006). In this way, assessment has become a practice that is fundamental to effective teaching and learning.

Now standards have been introduced into New Zealand schools, leaving many school leaders and teachers wondering whether this is a good or bad idea. How do they link to the Curriculum? What possibilities are there for using them as a source of evidence for improving teaching and learning? Whatever their views, New Zealand school leaders and teachers are now in the position of having to take account of standards in reading, writing and mathematics in their work.

Standards have been introduced in many countries as a way to provide greater clarity for politicians, parents, teachers and school leaders about what students are expected to be able to do at various points in their schooling. They have also been the subject of considerable debate, and it would be fair to say that most of the debate has focused on the negative impact of standards as they have been implemented, particularly in the United States (e.g., Glass, 2008). This negativity has arisen because the type of standards, the associated assessments and the uses to which they have been put in many states have resulted in a narrowing of the curriculum and excessive time being spent in test preparation, together with punitive consequences for those students, teachers and schools who have not met the standards (e.g., Dorn, 2007; Nicols & Berliner, 2007).

It is reasonable to ask, therefore, why we would write a book that weaves together evidence, inquiry and *standards*. Part of our motivation for putting this book together is to try to avert the kinds of negative consequences experienced in many other countries and to optimise the chances that standards will be used to promote the kinds of learning that are valued in the *Curriculum* through using the rich descriptions that accompany the standards as a source of information for advancing teaching and learning. This will only happen, however, if professional and community learning—rather than punitive accountability—remain to the fore.

We need to sound a note of caution, however. Although the focus of this book is how standards and their related assessment can be used as a source of evidence for inquiry into the effectiveness of practice, as researchers we have no control over the way in which standards might be used by governments and ministries of education. We recognise the risks many have claimed. In the meantime, we consider that the introduction of standards into the New Zealand education system has provided an opportunity to steer their use into those purposes that serve the needs of schools, parents and students, and we hope to promote this idea through writing this book. We also need to note that weaving standards into current systems of school review and action is not fundamentally different from the kinds of effective practice in which many schools already engage.

The remainder of this chapter describes how we see the place of evidence and inquiry in building better schools, and how standards fit into the picture. We conclude with a brief discussion on leading change, because of its fundamental place in the process of improvement.

Using evidence for inquiry

One of the distinguishing features of New Zealand education has been the promotion of inquiry as fundamental to effective professional practice, as evident in *The New Zealand Curriculum* (Ministry of Education, 2007b). We see this professional focus as being a strength of our system. What may be its weakness, however, is a problem identified by Michael Fullan (2007): although words travel well, their underlying concepts and thinking may not. We therefore begin this section by outlining what we mean by "inquiry" and how the use of evidence is fundamental to that process.

At its most basic, inquiry in schools is a process in which those involved investigate what is working well for student learning and achievement and why, so it can be continued, and what is not working well and why, so it can be changed. Timperley, Wilson, Barrar, and Fung (2008) developed this basic idea into an inquiry and knowledge-building cycle. Engagement in this cycle has been shown to result in improved outcomes for students. It has been adapted for this book to include both school leaders and teachers because of their joint responsibility, in partnership with parents, for student learning (see Figure 1.1).

The cycle begins by asking about students' learning needs in relation to the kinds of outcomes that are valued, such as those identified in *The New Zealand Curriculum*. The inquiry then moves on to asking leaders and teachers about their professional strengths and learning needs in relation to the educational experiences they need to provide for their students if they are to make adequate progress on those outcomes. Identification of the relevant professional skills and knowledge then forms the basis for engaging in professional learning experiences designed to meet these needs. As a result of such engagement, new learning experiences are provided for students, which are then tested for their impact.

Figure 1.1 Building knowledge through cycles of professional inquiry

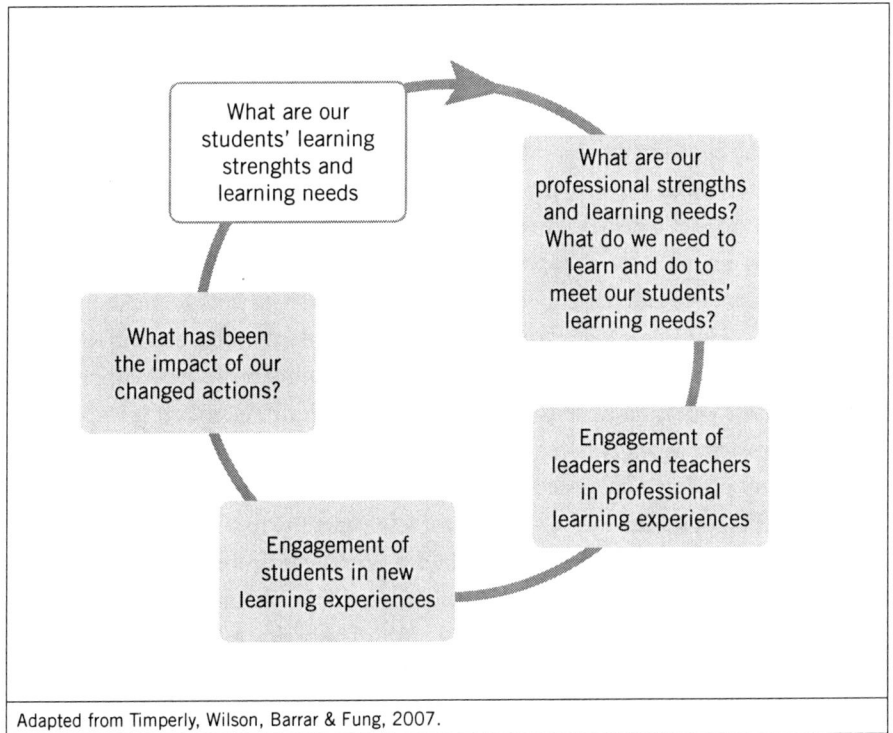

What are our students' learning strenghts and learning needs

What are our professional strengths and learning needs? What do we need to learn and do to meet our students' learning needs?

What has been the impact of our changed actions?

Engagement of leaders and teachers in professional learning experiences

Engagement of students in new learning experiences

Adapted from Timperly, Wilson, Barrar & Fung, 2007.

Engagement in this cycle requires a range of evidence-related capabilities. To find out what students are learning well and what they need to learn requires detailed assessment information that tells school leaders and teachers what students know in relation to the *Curriculum* and what they need to learn and do to make further progress. Checking impact requires similar information. The assessments that are used, however, must be fit-for-purpose and allow appropriate diagnoses to be made. Information about students who are making good progress is unlikely to need the same level of detail as for those who are doing less well. Engagement in assessment rituals whereby all students are assessed year after year in the same way without careful consideration of purpose is unlikely to meet the demands of the diagnosis task.

Evidence is also needed to identify professional strengths and learning needs, and to link these to the strengths and needs of the students. To use this kind of evidence, leaders and teachers must consider how they have contributed to existing student outcomes, what they already know they can use to promote the outcomes valued and what they need to learn and do to meet the needs of those students not achieving so well. This kind of evidence focuses on depth of professional knowledge and effectiveness of practice. Evidence is also needed of changes in the learning experiences of students to ensure these changes promote the kind of engagement intended.

> Evidence refers
> to more than
> student learning.
> It also includes
> professional
> knowledge and
> practices, and what
> is known about
> making the most
> difference.

Another form of evidence concerns what is known about how to make the most difference to student learning, particularly for those students not achieving as well in our system as their peers. This evidence relates to knowing *why* particular practices work or do not work, because unless the reasons are understood, it is impossible to identify exactly what it is that needs to be maintained and what needs to be changed. Any professional practice is highly complex and is not simply replicated in a new setting in its entirety. Over the last few years the research evidence about the approaches most likely to work—and why—for these underachieving students has grown considerably. Many of the authors in this book have been involved in this research in New Zealand (e.g., Lai et al., 2009; Timperley & Parr, 2009), building on the knowledge of others internationally. Understanding the implications of this body of research requires new learning for leaders and teachers.

The view we take of teachers and leaders engaging in evidence-informed inquiry to build better schools is very different from that of many other approaches. Rather than viewing teachers as experts in routines of professional practice, we view them as adaptive experts who retrieve, organise and apply professional knowledge when old problems persist or new problems arise. They have the capability to work out when the old routines do not work and to integrate new information to take different approaches when needed (Bransford, Derry, Berliner, & Hammerness, 2005). Similarly, our view of schools is one of leaders acting in a similar way. These leaders maintain routines when these work, but know when they need to expand the depth and breadth of current expertise.

The ability to use this kind of evidence for inquiry and improvement by adaptive experts is sometimes referred to as *evaluative capability*. This term has been described by many of those we work with as "a bit of a mouthful". Essentially, however, it captures the notion that to be effective in building better schools, school leaders, teachers, parents and students need to develop the knowledge and skills to undertake a series of activities including:

• establishing which outcomes are sufficiently valued by those involved to justify the focus and effort
• identifying the information needed to work out how to judge progress towards these outcomes
• developing a shared understanding of the conditions that might be limiting student learning and achievement
• making an informed selection and taking courses of action that address these conditions
• checking progress (both the rate and level) towards the valued outcomes, and making appropriate adjustments to relevant activities
• ensuring that all those who need to know have timely and accessible information about student learning and achievement
• embedding these evaluative activities as a socialised practice for all participants within the schooling improvement community.

These capabilities are central to building better schools. Indeed, much of the material included in this book has arisen from a set of position papers the authors have brought together through their research and evaluation work with schools involved in schooling improvement.

Standards in the New Zealand context

Recently, standards have been introduced into this mix of evidence and inquiry. In essence, the standards provide reference points for school leaders, teachers, parents and students to help make judgements about students' progress in relation to *The New Zealand Curriculum* and to make decisions about future actions. What adjustments to practice are needed? Is formal intervention required? The reason for focusing the standards on reading, writing and mathematics is that these learning areas are fundamental to accessing the *Curriculum* fully. In order to understand whether students are meeting particular standards, teachers are being asked to make an overall judgement on student achievement and progress. Seen in this light, the standards and the relevant assessment information gathered to make judgements about them are simply another form of evidence. Whether or not this process will lead to professional learning to build better schools depends on the support teachers are given to make the judgements required and the uses to which the evidence is put.

As with any assessment process, information about how well individuals and groups of students meet the standards can be used for compliance and reporting, with the accompanying sense of relief that one more task is thereby completed. Alternatively (and hopefully), the information will be used more formatively to help school leaders and teachers engage in the inquiry and knowledge-building process illustrated in Figure 1.1. Schools with effective self-review systems have engaged in similar processes for a long time.

What the standards can do is add to the mix of information about expected levels of achievement and students' progress towards them. This information is needed to answer the question "What are our students' learning needs in relation to valued outcomes?" The standards themselves—and the accompanying resources, such as exemplars and explanations—provide specific and rich descriptions of expected achievement profiles in relation to the *Curriculum*. These descriptions can help school leaders, teachers and parents to understand what it is their students should be learning and doing if they are to meet the expectations of the *Curriculum*. Rigorous assessment of students' progress against the standards, like any other diagnostically framed assessment information, can provide details of students' learning profiles and help to identify any gaps between what is expected and what is happening. This information can also serve as a reference point for assessing the impact of change.

The process of change

Knowing about expectations and identifying gaps involve a process of change if better schools are to be built. Otherwise evidence and inquiry will simply preserve the status quo. Many books have been written about leading and managing change, which we cannot hope to summarise in a few pages. There are, however, some key principles that underpin the ideas throughout this book, which we outline below.

In his book on *School Reform from the Inside Out*, Elmore (2004) stresses the importance of any change affecting the instructional core:

> By the 'core of educational practice,' I mean how teachers understand the nature of knowledge and the student's role in learning, and how these ideas about knowledge and learning are manifested in teaching and classwork. The 'core' also includes structural

arrangements of schools, such as the physical layout of classrooms, student grouping practices, teachers' responsibilities for groups of students, and relations among teachers in their work with students, as well as processes for assessing student learning and communicating it to students, teachers, parents, administrators, and other interested parties. (p. 8)

Some of these activities, such as assessing student learning and communicating the information, involve working with the standards and other relevant evidence directly. Other activities are more distant from the instructional core, such as reporting to the community. If leaders and teachers are to learn how to improve practice as a result of analysing students' progress on and access to the *Curriculum* by referencing the standards or other evidence, then all these activities are highly relevant. The change involved in building better schools requires more than assessing and reporting.

Another principle on which we have focused in this book involves identifying what parts of this instructional core are most and least likely to be having an impact on student outcomes, and then focusing on those that are most promising. There is so much going on in schools at any one time that it is sometimes difficult to identify what is working and what is not. Some initiatives and instructional approaches continue for years with little impact. Others are short term and layered on top of other improvement efforts, leaving little opportunity for an evaluation of their effects. The result is often burnt-out teachers trying to cope with all the change initiatives, with the same groups of children continuing to achieve poorly. One way to work through this issue is to identify and select interventions with a strong evidence base of effectiveness when assessment information indicates a change in direction is needed.

> For change to be effective, it must have an impact on the instructional core, but teachers cannot accomplish change alone.

When considering which of these high-impact initiatives to select, it is important to ensure that their underlying approaches to instruction and meaning making are coherent with what has gone before; that is, they should be based on similar principles. O'Connell (2009) found that schools in New Zealand that ensured new initiatives built on an understanding of previous work were better able to sustain high achievement gains for students in literacy. Teachers benefited because they deepened their knowledge and could see how approaches to teaching and assessing literacy, for example, applied to numeracy. Students benefited because they experienced similar

> No-one should be blamed during the process of building better schools, but all must take responsibility for improvement.

teaching approaches, even though the subject content changed. Jumping from one idea to the next, or including them all, leads to superficial understandings, shallow implementation and initiative overload. Discontinuity of direction creates distractions and undermines teacher motivation and feelings of being in control.

Part of feeling out of control in situations of change is that those responsible for implementing new ideas do not necessarily understand what it is they are supposed to be implementing. Elmore (2004) claims that one of the strongest social norms in schools is that everyone is expected to pretend they are equally effective in what they do, even when they feel they are unprepared to do it. Explicit capability building is not seen to be part of the change agenda. In the case of initiatives like the introduction of a new curriculum and the standards, capability building is central to success if these initiatives are to be a force for change. Nobody should have to pretend.

This capability building must be for the purpose of making *meaning*, not just for implementing particular requirements (Fullan, 2007). Mandates without knowledge create fear and anxiety and are demotivating—as much for leaders as for teachers. Some of the understanding required in order to use the standards to build better schools, for example, will involve leaders and teachers:

- knowing the standards and being competent in interpreting information from various sources to make overall teacher judgements
- knowing how to use the information to engage in professional inquiry processes
- knowing how to work with others (professional colleagues, parents and students) to create improvement.

A learning, problem-solving focus for all those involved, rather than a compliance focus, is most likely to lead to professional and organisational learning with better outcomes for those students whose education needs are less well met than others in the system. No one should be blamed, but all need to take responsibility for solving identified problems and for inquiring into their impact on student learning and achievement. The research that identifies that teachers make the difference (Alton-Lee, 2003; Hattie, 2009) has received a great deal of recent publicity. While it is certainly teachers who are central to student learning, they cannot do it alone. A recent Best Evidence Synthesis Iteration on school leadership (Robinson, Hōhepa, & Lloyd, 2009) identified that the leadership activities with the greatest impact on student outcomes involved the leaders' promotion of and participation in professional development of the teachers. For leaders to exercise this role, they and their teachers need support from the education system. This support is wide ranging and includes access to expertise and the conditions to make use of it. Making a difference is difficult work and requires much more than simply making changes to teaching practice.

It is possible to engage in all the activities outlined above and not make much difference to student outcomes, because change for improvement involves complex processes requiring subtleties in their application. We finish this section by briefly describing a study in the United Kingdom involving teachers from schools with contrasting success in adding value to student achievement (Hay Group Management Ltd, 2004). Teachers ranked 30 statements according to whether they agreed they were true/right for their school. Teachers from both high and lower value-added schools ranked "Measuring and monitoring of targets and results" as their top item. It seems, therefore, that this activity is a necessary, although not a sufficient, condition for improvement. Other items provided better contrasts. While the teachers from the high value-added schools ranked items about raising capability, helping people learn and laying foundations for later success at the top of their lists, teachers from the lower value-added schools gave greater weight to warmth, humour and creating a pleasant and collegial working environment. Similarly, teachers from the higher value-added schools referred to a hunger for improvement, with high hopes and expectations, including promoting excellence. In contrast, their lower value-added counterparts were more focused on recognising personal circumstances and focusing on effort rather than outcomes. Developing capability, helping people learn and creating high hopes and expectations form the core of this book.

About this book

This book comprises a series of theme-based chapters containing key ideas we have found to be important for schools in our research into professional learning and schooling improvement. Each chapter contains a set of propositions related to the theme of the chapter, which the schools in which we have been working have found useful in guiding their thinking. Most chapters illustrate these propositions by describing a continuum of development that illustrates the practices related to a proposition or theme in schools just beginning their improvement efforts and operating at a basic level, how these efforts might evolve into a middle or mixed level of operation and what they might look like at a more integrated level. This continuum is designed to help schools to locate their current development level—wherever that may be—and to track their progress through their individual journeys.

In our experience, schools don't jump from basic to integrated levels in one giant leap. Nor is their profile across, or even within, themes consistently at one level: they are always more advanced at some aspects than others. Knowing something, including how to undertake the difficult work of schooling improvement, has a developmental history that requires the careful and systematic building of structures, processes and knowledge, and takes time and persistence. Levin (2008) refers to this process as the "slog work of implementation" (p. 6), because in something as multifaceted as schooling improvement instant transformations are rare. These progressions have been checked with school leaders engaged in the process of change. Their feedback has indicated that they provide a kind of road map for schools that provides direction and helps prevent taking "no exit" roads and unnecessary detours, thus shortening the time taken to move through the process.

This book is not a step-by-step guide on how to build better schools, with accompanying steps or programmes. It will not answer questions like, "Should a teacher use a particular instructional strategy to address certain identified learning problems?" or "How often should principals visit school classrooms?" To suggest that such questions can be answered in the abstract, for all schools, belittles the complexities of any schooling improvement endeavour, much of which is determined by the local context in which a school operates. Instead, the book focuses on building adaptive expertise throughout schools.

This said, some important ideas do apply across contexts, and it is these that are highlighted in this book. They focus on the mix of evidence, inquiry and standards. Each chapter outlines the issues that need to be taken into consideration when thinking about the theme of the chapter, which can then serve as a reference for school leaders and teachers for what they should take into account when thinking about using evidence-informed inquiry to build better schools.

The book is divided into three parts. The first part provides an overview of the big picture and consists of this introductory chapter and Chapter Two, which has the title "Towards an Optimal Model for Building Better Schools". This chapter provides an overview of some core concepts relevant to efforts towards schooling improvement. One of the core concepts is *capability*, which means having the knowledge and skills to carry out specific roles, responsibilities and actions required to improve student outcomes. Important dimensions of capability are instructional, organisational and evaluative capability, and these dimensions are elaborated in Chapter Two. A second core concept is *relationships*. Relationships with outside agencies or other levels of the system are needed in order to effect improvement. Where there is complementarity and mutually informed learning, we have referred to this relationship as *managed interdependence*. Relationships among those within the school are about building trust while challenging one another to improve.

The second part is focused on preparing for change and comprises Chapters Three to Five. Chapter Three, co-authored by Mei Lai, Helen Timperley, and Stuart McNaughton, examines theories for improvement and sustainability. The purpose of this chapter is to provide a working guide that clearly explains the concept of theories for improvement and sustainability, and their value to schools. These theories underpin all school practices, including those involved in change. Understanding, in terms of knowing how to develop productive theories and evaluating those theories, should enable schools to design more effective practices to improve and sustain valued student outcomes.

Chapter Four, entitled "Changing Tack: Talking about Change Knowledge for Professional Learning", by Deidre Le Fevre, elaborates on the theme of change. Talking about change is central to the improvement process. This chapter addresses issues related to the reasons for talking about change, the ways in which change should be prioritised, highlighting expectations for change, the challenges of change and evaluating change. The progressions identified in the change process relate to these particular dimensions.

Chapter Five, by Margie Hōhepa, examines issues related to learning and inquiry in Māori-medium education. Māori-medium education has been a somewhat neglected poor cousin in an English-medium environment, whereby teachers in Māori medium have been expected to adapt practices developed in English medium to their situation. How this might be addressed in mixed schooling contexts made up of Māori- and English-medium settings is discussed in this chapter. Recently a cluster of kura kaupapa Māori schools have engaged in schooling improvement, and the implications for Māori-medium-only schools is considered in light of this experience.

Part Three is focused on inquiry using evidence, and comprises Chapters Six to Eight. Chapter Six, by Judy Parr, examines the kinds of inquiry in classrooms that are integral to informing teaching and learning. In a standards environment, where the notion of overall teacher judgement operates in order to decide whether a student is meeting a standard, the capability of teachers to select, weigh and integrate appropriate information from a range of sources to form this judgement is crucial. This chapter examines the process. The focus is not simply on the capability of teachers to know their students. It also includes evaluating their students' learning and progress in order to make strategic use of this information in relation to their own practice. The chapter also directs attention to teachers' capability in terms of enabling their students to self-evaluate and become self-regulating learners.

Analysing student achievement data is central to the improvement process but is not always undertaken in ways that allow certain judgements about student achievement level and progress to be made. Chapter Seven, by Rachel Dingle and Judy Parr, examines issues related to this task. Many schools collect, enter and analyse achievement data during a particular school year reasonably accurately. While the chapter will briefly cover these issues for schools not yet at this stage, a focus will be on understanding issues related to the importance of value-added longitudinal analysis of these data, because it is becoming increasingly clear that it is important to assess improvement efforts in this light. The essence of the chapter will be an overview of what comprises quality data about valued outcomes of student learning, so that judgements can be made about that learning to inform schools' efforts to improve.

Chapter Eight, by Mei Lai and Stuart McNaughton, outlines the kinds of conversations about data that can have a positive impact on student achievement. Schools are becoming increasingly focused on collecting and using data for improvement purposes. Interpretive conversations are central to school leaders' and teachers' ability to use the data well, and this will form the focus of the chapter. Important dimensions of interpersonal relationships, the quality of the data and the willingness of participants to learn from data will be introduced. The main focus of the chapter, however, is on how school-based conversations can build knowledge for teaching when the participants engage with the data.

The book concludes with a final chapter by the editors, which weaves together the themes of evidence, inquiry and standards into building better schools for the future. To help illustrate this, a series of cases is presented. They show how schools with different profiles, assessed by evaluating themselves using the progressions contained in these chapters, make choices about how best to proceed.

References

Alton-Lee, A. (2003). *Quality teaching for diverse students in schooling.* Wellington: Ministry of Education. Retrieved from http://educationcounts.edcentre. govt.nz/goto/BES

Bransford, J., Derry, S., Berliner, D., & Hammerness, I. (2005). Theories of learning and their roles in teaching. In L. Darling-Hammond & J. Bransford (Eds.), *Preparing teachers for a changing world* (pp. 40–87). San Francisco: John Wiley & Sons.

Dorn, S. (2007). *Accountability Frankenstein: Understanding and taming the monster.* Charlotte, NC: Information Age Publishing.

Elmore, R. (2004). *School reform from the inside out: Policy, practice and performance.* Cambridge, MA: Harvard Education Press.

Fullan, M. (2007). *The new meaning of educational change.* New York: Teachers College Press.

Glass, G. V. (2008). *Fertilizers, pills and magnetic strips: The fate of public education in America.* Charlotte, NC: Information Age Publishing.

Hattie, J. (2009). *Visible learning: A synthesis of over 800 meta-analyses relating to achievement.* London, New York: Routledge.

Hay Group Management Ltd. (2004). *A culture for learning.* London: Author.

Lai, M., McNaughton, S., Timperley, H., & Hsiao, S. (2009). Sustaining continued acceleration in reading comprehension achievement following an intervention. *Educational Assessment, Evaluation and Accountability, 32*(1), 81–100.

Levin, B. (2008). *How to change 5000 schools.* Cambridge, MA: Harvard Education Press.

Ministry of Education. (2007a). *Te marautanga o Aotearoa: He tauira hei kōrerorero.* Wellington: Learning Media.

Ministry of Education. (2007b). *The New Zealand curriculum.* Wellington: Learning Media.

Nicols, S. L., & Berliner, D. C. (2007). *Collateral damage: How high stakes testing corrupts America's schools.* Cambridge, MA: Harvard Education Press.

O'Connell, P. (2009). *Is sustainability of schooling improvement an article of faith or can it be deliberately crafted?* Unpublished doctoral thesis, The University of Auckland, Auckland.

Robinson, V., Hōhepa, M., & Lloyd, C. (2009). *School leadership and student outcomes: Identifying what works and why: A best evidence synthesis.* Wellington: Ministry of Education.

Timperley, H., & Parr, J. (2009). Chain of influence from policy to practice in the New Zealand Literacy Strategy. *Research Papers in Education, 24*(2), 135–154.

Timperley, H., Wilson, A., Barrar, H., & Fung, I. (2007). *Teacher professional learning and development: A best evidence synthesis iteration.* Wellington: Ministry of Education.

Wiliam, D. (2006). Assessment: Learning communities can use it to engineer a bridge connecting teaching and learning. *Journal of Staff Development, 27*(1), 16–20.

CHAPTER TWO

Towards an Optimal Model for Building Better Schools

Helen Timperley, Stuart McNaughton, Mei Lai,
Margie Hōhepa, Judy Parr and Rachel Dingle

Chapter One described the knowledge-building and inquiry cycle for teachers, leaders and those offering systemic support to schools (see Figure 1.1). In this chapter we present a model that integrates the inquiry and knowledge-building cycles with three important capabilities that we have found in our collective work to be essential for teachers and school leaders to build better schools when using evidence for inquiry purposes (Figure 2.1). The capabilities are instructional, organisational and evaluative, and develop through engagement in the kinds of inquiry that systematically build knowledge.

Relationships are also essential to building these capabilities and are part of the model. The relationships we have highlighted are managed interdependence with those with specialist expertise, together with trust and challenge in relation to those involved in improvement efforts. The chapter concludes with descriptions of a continuum of typical activities involving evidence-informed inquiry and identifies what these two core concepts might look like in practice.

Figure 2.1 Towards an Optimal Model for Building Better Schools

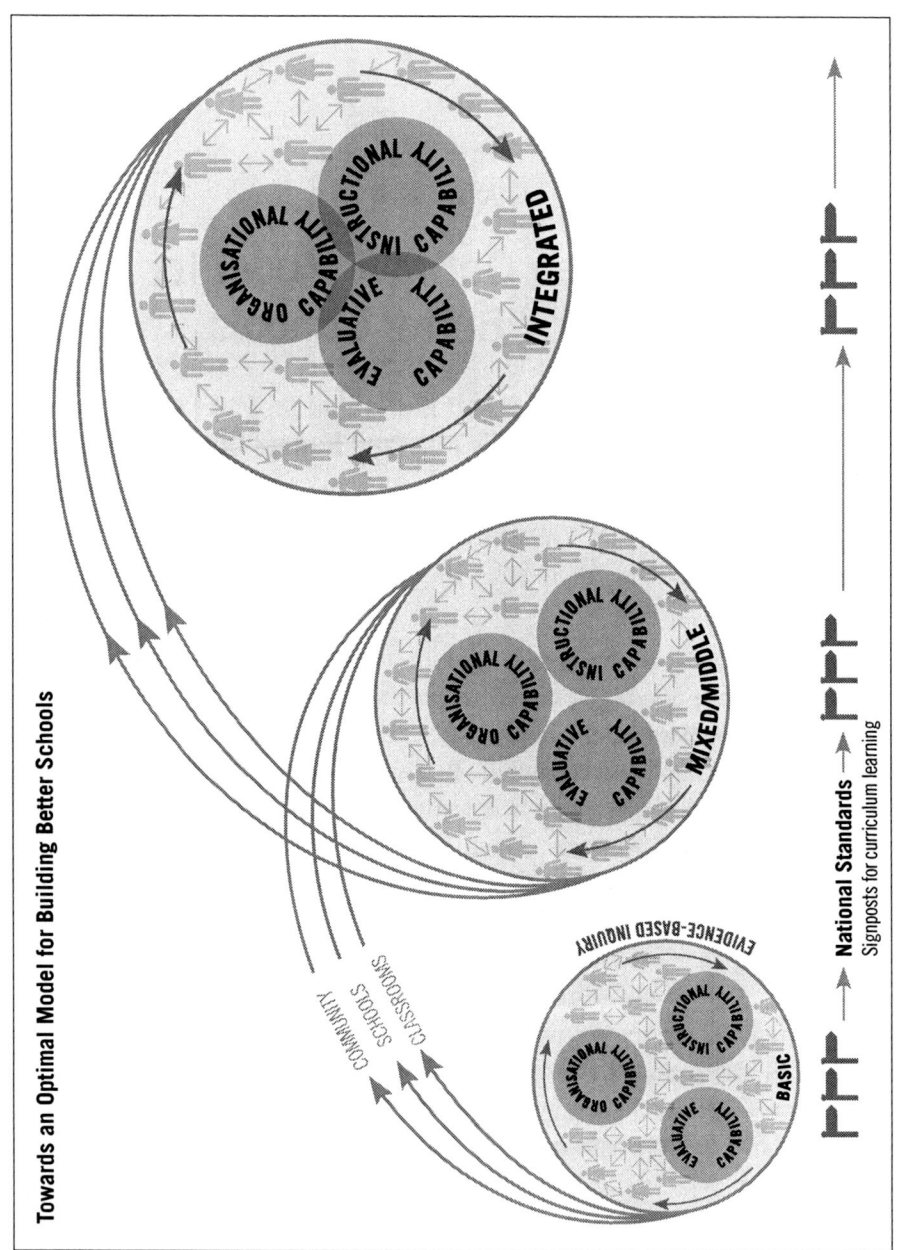

The model

Inquiry, as described it in Chapter One, is fundamental to building better schools. Thus, in the model presented in Figure 2.1, the large circles represent cycles of evidence-informed inquiry that focus on building knowledge and skills for the purpose of developing instructional, organisational and evaluative capabilities at all levels of the system. Fundamental to the inquiry cycle is the idea that students and their learning form the focus of all improvement efforts, whether the inquirer is a teacher, school leader, family/whānau or policy maker. Students' progress and achievement are the reasons to engage in professional learning, with success decided on the basis of progress on the outcomes valued by the school community.

The focus of professional learning to address teachers' and leaders' learning needs is determined by what they need to know and do, mainly in terms of instructional capability for their students to make accelerated progress on these outcomes. This focus is of particular importance for those students not achieving well in our education system. These inquiry cycles can be part of daily classroom practice, or they can operate on a longer term basis. An example of day-by-day use of the cycle might be when a teacher notices that a student is not grasping a particular concept, and so he or she knocks on the door of a neighbouring teacher to discuss what happened and together they consult resources and pool knowledge to work out what is best to do next. The first teacher then tries out the new practice and checks the student's work to find out if their understanding has improved. Alternatively, the cycles can occur over a much longer time frame, whereby students' profiles of achievement at the middle of the year are compared with those at the beginning of the year. Organisational capability might need to be developed so that routines associated with assessment are embedded within the school.

Three ascending inquiry cycles are depicted in Figure 2.1, because knowing how to do something has a developmental history. Schools as organisations, for example, take time to develop, then learn how to integrate the instructional, organisational and evaluative capabilities. This idea is shown by the smaller and separate, nonoverlapping circles within the inquiry cycles in the early stages. As occurs with students, knowing something at an organisational level in such a way that it can be integrated with other knowledge and skills takes time and practice. Each of these aspects of the model is further unpacked in the remainder of this chapter, drawing on both the details of the inquiry cycles in Figure 1.1 and the wider concepts in Figure 2.1.

The relationship between the capabilities and the inquiry cycle is synergistic. The capabilities are partly built through engaging in inquiry and the outcomes of that inquiry, and inquiry, in turn, is strengthened by enhanced capability.

Capability

By capability we mean having the knowledge and skills to carry out the specific roles, responsibilities and actions needed to improve student outcomes. Describing these capabilities alone could fill this book, so we have selected just three to elaborate here. They include instructional, organisational and evaluative capabilities.

Instructional capability

This capability involves the knowledge and skills required to select and use effective instructional practices to meet the needs of particular groups of students. Our knowledge of what constitutes effective instructional practices has evolved in recent times. In particular, we have moved from identifying generic practices likely to be effective, to the notion of the teacher as adaptive expert who is able to identify, tailor or construct the specific practice that works for particular student needs in a given context. As a result, the demands involved in instructional capability are high, particularly when trying to accelerate the progress of those students achieving less well in our schools.

> Instructional capability involves the knowledge and skills required to select and use effective instructional practices for particular groups of students.

Identifying what it is that students know and can do, and what they need to know and do to make progress, relies on having individual profiles of learning and achievement. Not all practices are equally effective for all students. Sometimes classroom practices effective for high-achieving students are not as effective for their lower achieving peers, and vice versa. Knowing about effective instruction, therefore, requires knowing learners' profiles of achievement and matching instructional approaches to their particular learning needs.

This differential impact of particular instructional practices also means that knowledge of teaching cannot be purely programmatic or technical. To be optimally effective, teachers are professional experts who are deeply knowledgeable about what they do, how they do it and why they do it. Their knowledge and skills are about particular instructional practices and how to assess students so as to understand their profiles of learning and achievement. They are able to integrate knowledge of assessment

> Teachers as adaptive experts retrieve, organise and apply professional knowledge to particular learning problems.

and instructional practices to develop specific forms of instructional guidance. They have knowledge and understanding of the domain of teaching, and of children and their learning that can be articulated. They understand how to teach effectively, and they have strategic practices that are versatile and adaptable (McNaughton & Lai, 2009). Adaptive expertise, whereby teachers retrieve, organise and apply professional knowledge to particular learning problems, is central to effectiveness (Bransford, Derry, Berliner, & Hammerness, 2005). Such knowledge is principled. It requires an understanding of the rationale for particular practices.

CASE STUDY 2.1

Let's take the case of a teacher, Sally, wanting to develop the knowledge and writing skills needed to produce a rich description recounting the experience of being caught in a storm, as there had recently been just such a sudden, unseasonal storm in the area. Although all the students experienced the storm, recounting this for some simply involved a litany of events: it began to rain hard, it was windy too, and we ran to get shelter, grabbing all the food and rugs etc. They may not have thought of describing the experience through all of their senses. For some students, the reading of a model text cued this approach; others required that specific features of the text were pointed out so that they understood how the author created the feeling of being chilled to the bone in the reader, and so on. Some needed additional help with particular vocabulary. However, for other students, the most effective approach was not a model text, but an experience or series of experiences—real or simulated—with talk that introduced appropriate descriptive words and rehearsed shared experiences; for example, what it felt like to be in the wind on a wet, blustery day.

For each of these groups of students the teacher may be drawing on the same content knowledge of how the language and structure of recount operates, but Sally also has to draw on professional knowledge (of pedagogy and of students) to adapt to the differing needs of the students in the class.

An alternative view of what it is to be a teacher is having the technical capability to implement prespecified programmes developed by others. Teacher and school development programmes that arise from this view may raise achievement in the short term but don't guarantee sustainability of ongoing improvements to instructional practices over the longer term. Indeed, focusing on technical, instructional capability alone may limit further problem solving because the emphasis is on the fidelity of programme implementation rather than whether the programme or approach is addressing the particular needs of *these* students at *this* time.

Organisational capability

Although effective instructional practice is central to the kinds of outcomes desired for students, teachers cannot build better schools on their own. Those who work in schools that are organised to maximise instructional time and to systematically develop teachers' instructional capability acknowledge these aspects as central to their success. Clearly, leadership is central to organisational capability.

As knowledge of effective instruction has developed rapidly in recent years, so has knowledge of leadership and organisational capability. Understanding of teachers as adaptive experts demands that the school as an organisation operates in a similar way (Lai, McNaughton, Timperley, & Hsiao, 2009). It has long been recognised that effective organisations are those that balance the routine with the innovative so that they avoid the problems of stagnation or being overwhelmed by change (March, 1996). Adaptive expertise within an organisation requires systems to identify what is working well and therefore should remain, and what is not working so well and so needs to change. It also involves a well-developed, more conceptual understanding of the reasons why systems work well or not so well.

> Organisations with adaptive expertise have systems to identify what is working well and should remain, and what is not working so well so needs to change.

Professional learning at all levels of the school is central to the development of this kind of expertise. As mentioned in Chapter One, in a recent synthesis of the kinds of leadership practices that have a high impact on student learning, Robinson, Hōhepa, and Lloyd (2009) identified that leadership involvement in promoting and participating in teacher professional development had the greatest effects. These kinds of activities potentially link leader and teacher professional learning, thus enhancing organisational capability. Through their participation, leaders come to know their "class of teachers" as teachers come to know their class of students. Teachers are as diverse in their learning needs as their students and should not have to pretend they know what they have not had the opportunity to learn.

One reason this book does not take the form of a step-by-step guide is that developing organisational capability requires understanding the principles underlying particular capabilities and adapting them to particular contexts. Ensuring these adaptations work in a particular context requires a third kind of capability, which we have identified as *evaluative capability*.

Evaluative capability

Given the difficulty of defining exactly which instructional and organisational practices meet the needs of which particular students, the capability to evaluate the effectiveness of particular activities in an ongoing way is central. Without this capability, Katz, Earl, and Ben Jafaar (2009) argue that schools can end up in "activity traps". In other words, they engage in many well-intentioned activities that are not truly needs based and have the effect of diverting resources away from where they are most necessary.

Evaluative capability requires using evidence throughout the teaching and learning cycles so that those involved can answer the questions "Where am I going?", "How am I doing?" and "Where to next" (Hattie & Timperley, 2007). Sometimes it is assumed that evaluation simply involves looking at achievement results and deciding what next. Evaluative capability requires much more. It involves identifying what outcomes for students are desired and necessary, and the type of information needed to work out how to make judgements about attainment and progress. It also involves the capability to develop a shared understanding of the conditions that may be limiting professional and student learning, taking specific actions to address those conditions, checking the impact of these actions in terms of what is desired and engaging in further cycles of inquiry. Each of these dimensions is described below.

> Evaluative capability requires the use of evidence to answer the questions "Where am I going?", "How am I going?" and "Where to next?"

First, it is important to decide what outcomes are desired so that those with an interest (students, parents, whānau, teachers and leaders) can judge whether the progress achieved is adequate. This is where well designed standards have the potential to guide consideration, and exemplify at least a subset of desired outcomes at different levels. Nearly all students make progress. The key question, particularly for those students not achieving well in our education system, is whether that progress is sufficient for them to catch up to their peers in relation to the outcomes valued by the community. This judgement is an integral part of the inquiry and knowledge-building cycle.

Part of the decision about outcomes is to ensure they are situated within the *Curriculum*, such that the *Curriculum* is seen as the overarching umbrella. One of the dangers in a standards environment, in particular, is that the standards become the default curriculum, thus leading to the curriculum becoming narrowed. The standards are only reference points in reading, writing and mathematics and should not be substituted for a much richer curriculum across a number of domains.

Second, identifying the information needed to work out how to make judgements about progress is required. In the new environment of national standards, the importance of multiple sources of data is emphasised. Externally benchmarked assessments should form part of the picture because they help school leaders, teachers, parents and whānau to take a broad view of the progress and achievement of their students in terms of expected progress. Judgements about progress should also be informed by teachers', parents' and whānau knowledge of students and how they work and learn in varying contexts, in and out of school.

For many outcomes there are no externally referenced assessments, so more thought and planning are needed. For example, in Māori-medium-education settings, students' mastery of te reo Māori is central to the kaupapa of the schools and community. Working out what information is needed to decide if students are moving towards mastery and how to make overall teacher judgements are essential for gauging progress.

> Evaluative capability includes developing a shared understanding of the conditions that may be limiting professional and student learning.

An important aspect of evaluative capability is to develop a shared understanding of the conditions within the school and particular classrooms that may be limiting professional and student learning, and relate this to the question in the second box of the inquiry cycles, "What are our professional strengths and learning needs?" (see Figure 1.1). The purpose of undertaking this kind of exercise is not to blame anyone, but to learn about what needs to change. It is also important to ensure there are no "off limits" in discussion. If teachers find some aspects of the leadership of the school are limiting their ability to learn and teach, for example, this issue needs to be discussed and resolved. One example of something that teachers feel limits their ability to teach is when administrative interruptions occur throughout the school day, such as notices over the intercom and messages arriving from "the office". An expectation can develop that these administrative demands should take priority over teaching and learning, even though all would agree that it is the instructional time that makes the difference to student outcomes. The challenge for teachers is to let leaders know about the negative consequences of the interruptions. The challenge for leaders is to find alternative ways to meet organisational demands that do not have unintended negative outcomes.

Another off-limits issue can be the depth of teacher knowledge and skills in particular aspects of practice. With knowledge changing as rapidly as it is, diversity in particular knowledge and skills should be expected and accepted. Yet a strong social norm is often to pretend that all are equally skilled (Elmore, 2004). Such pretence only increases teachers' stress and does little to develop essential knowledge and skills for improvement. Talking about change and what is required to achieve such change is an essential element in the process. This issue is further discussed in Chapter Four.

CASE STUDY 2.2

Fortunately for Sally, our teacher wanting to utilise the recent storm experience to teach writing, particularly the idea of a recount that captures the intensity of an event, the syndicate and school did not have a structure that meant implementing a lock-step programme, whereby everyone had to cover certain things at certain times. As a result she was able to move easily into recount writing. The resulting pieces of work were vivid and of a high standard. However, when the next whole-school assessment was conducted, the results were disappointing: the class had not transferred their high-quality recount writing to a piece requiring an argument. Moreover, across the school performance was not sufficiently high nor progress rapid enough to meet goals. In particular, boys were lagging behind (they do nationally, but this was a more extreme case). Looking across classes, much the same pattern was noted, particularly at Year 8.

Something needed to be changed in their collective writing programmes. This is where both instructional leadership and organisational capability are needed. The principal and literacy leader led teachers in a problem-solving exercise. They considered their knowledge of persuasive writing, testing what they knew against what research and other professional reading suggested were required. After consulting their records to see gaps and patterns in how each had gone about teaching this purpose for writing they came to a shared understanding of what appeared to be missing in their teaching of persuasive writing and what could be done.

Next, they invited an outside expert to give them feedback on the theory they had come up with regarding what was needed to aid transfer and, particularly, their ideas about the need for more focused teaching of argument: related sentence and text structures and vocabulary. They also asked for feedback on their plans for more student involvement in their learning, given that boys, in particular, have been shown to respond to a sense of autonomy and control. Together they planned how to implement these new practices, and also how they would monitor both whether they had mastered the changes they planned and whether these changes were more effective than previous practices.

Discussing and agreeing on the conditions that might be limiting learning is not enough: specific actions need to be taken to address these conditions. The key question to answer is, "What is believed to be causing what and how are we going to address it?" The process has parallels with assessing students. For too long the beginning of each school year has been taken up with extensive assessment exercises, only for teachers to breathe a sigh of relief when these are completed so that now they can get on with the teaching—without any close analysis of how that teaching should be shaped by the assessment information gathered. In the same way, it is important that having agreed on the conditions that might be limiting professional learning, everyone does not then breathe a sigh of relief and get on with the professional development plan that was agreed to the previous year, irrespective of the findings from the analysis of the limiting conditions. Intervention decisions, whether with students or teachers, need to be specific, targeted and focused on beliefs about causation. Through this specificity, these beliefs can be tested and revised if necessary. In Figure 1.1 this process is described as "Engagement of leaders and teachers in professional learning experiences" and "Engagement of students in new learning experiences".

> For interventions to be effective, they must be focused on addressing the agreed causes of the problem.

Although we know much more than we used to about how to focus leadership and teaching practices to address particular organisational and learning problems, schools are complex places. No particular course of action can be guaranteed to result in particular outcomes. For this reason, checking the implementation of agreed changes and their effectiveness in making progress towards the valued outcomes is central to evaluative capability. In Figure 1.1 of the inquiry and knowledge-building cycles, the question is "What has been the impact of our changed actions?" Earlier decisions about information needs might need to be revisited in the light of issues that have arisen and the information needs that have emerged as being important. Thus no part of the cycle is independent of any other. For some schools new information will be looked at for reporting in relation to the national standards. A key question for these schools is what information is required if all those who need to know (including parents, trustees, the community) get the kinds of information they will find useful?

Evaluating impact is unlikely to lead to ongoing improvement unless what is found out leads to another cycle of inquiry, knowledge building and changed practice, with new problems identified and new issues to solve. We have characterised this inquiry and knowledge-building process as requiring the development of organisational, instructional and evaluative capabilities. As the cycle repeats itself, these capabilities are further strengthened. In this way, evaluative capability becomes a socialised practice within the school.

Relationships

Developing instructional, organisational and evaluative capabilities in inquiry is not something an individual teacher, leader or school can do alone. Learning, teaching and leading are social activities. Professionals and parents/whānau work together to develop, trial and refine their knowledge and skills. We want to suggest that building better schools requires relationships of *managed interdependence* with those with specialist expertise, and relationships of *trust* and *challenge* with colleagues on the same journey.

Managed interdependence

Early in the life of change efforts, those involved often depend on external expertise for the necessary knowledge and skills. This is an almost inevitable part of the early stages of learning something new. The research literature (e.g., Bandura, 1995) suggests, however, that ongoing high dependence on external agents and/or other levels in the system may undermine effectiveness in terms of developing instructional, organisational and evaluative capability. Over time, too great a dependence can lead to a kind of "learned helplessness", where teachers and leaders do not develop the capability to make their own inquiries into whether their practice is working adequately.

> Managed interdependence involves complementary and mutually informed relationships with outside agencies with specialist expertise.

Independence on its own is also unlikely to lead to ongoing improvement and the development of key capabilities. As existing problems are solved, new ones emerge requiring different kinds of expertise to investigate and to address them. The early days of self-managing schools were based on the assumption that independence was something desirable, but over time its limitations to learning and development have become apparent. It is unrealistic to assume that schools can develop full autonomy in all the complex areas of expertise needed for improvement. Thus, we have referred in our optimal model (Figure 2.1) to a situation of managed interdependence. Managed interdependence involves developing complementary and mutually informed relationships with outside agencies with specialist expertise.

This kind of interdependence puts leaders and teachers in the driving seat of inquiry and change. As their instructional, organisational and evaluative capabilities are developed, they manage their relationships with outside agencies in terms of other system demands. They know, for example, when a new initiative offered by the Ministry of Education ties in with their current improvement efforts and builds on the professional learning plan developed for staff, and therefore whether it is likely to be of benefit to teachers and students alike. More importantly, they also know when to say "No". If what is offered has different theoretical underpinnings, then it is likely to overload staff, result in instructional fragmentation and reduce coherence within classroom programmes. Bryk and colleagues (1998) employed the term the "Christmas tree approach", whereby schools pick off the metaphorical tree presents that represent everything that is offered in the hope that something will work. What they found was that the students in these schools made less progress in literacy and numeracy than students in schools adopting a more coherent approach to change.

Managing interdependence with outside agencies and other levels of the system depends on having high levels of instructional, organisational and evaluative capability. Instructional capability is required to make decisions about the likely effectiveness of the particular approaches to learning and instruction being suggested. Is what is being offered by these agencies consistent with what is known about the likely worth of a particular pedagogical approach and its application to a particular curriculum domain? Is it theoretically consistent with what we have done or are doing that works well? Those with responsibility for developing organisational capability are likely to ask, "Is the likely benefit worth all the effort?" and "How does what is suggested fit with what we already do?" When evaluative capability is high, those involved are likely to demand information about the research supporting the claims made and evidence of effectiveness.

Trust and challenge

The interpersonal dynamics in any inquiry and change process influence success because the process of improving capability and developing interdependence is usually associated with a sense of vulnerability. Tony Bryk and colleagues (2007) in the United States have identified the importance of having a base level of trust, forged through day-to-day social exchanges, as being fundamental to success. Trust helps to develop

> Trust involves personal respect, integrity and carrying out mutual agreements.

buy-in, together with the motivation and deep engagement to undertake the difficult work of schooling improvement. These authors define trust in terms of personal respect, integrity and competence in the execution of basic responsibilities related to particular roles. This definition goes beyond the idea of trust as uncritical support of each other. It has a strong element of mutual accountability. Trust is based on perceptions of personal integrity that those involved can be trusted to keep their word and carry out mutual agreements. The specifics of how this looks in any particular situation will differ according to the cultural and contextual conditions.

Bryk and colleagues (2007) have also identified that the development of trust does not have a direct impact on student achievement. This impact results from the mutual learning that happens through having trust based on mutual respect. A dynamic of uncritical support, where everyone's contributions are taken as equally valid, does not promote such learning. It is likely that some participants have greater insights than others into particular situations. Blind spots for most of us happen when we are very closely involved. We need others to help us to see them. Social exchanges, therefore, need to include both understanding and *challenging* each other's claims, the beliefs underpinning them and the evidence on which they are based. Evidence and inquiry are at the centre of this process.

Challenge requires rigorous debate of the ideas put forward and the evidence that underpins them.

Trust develops from a perception that such challenges will be undertaken respectfully and in a supportive way. Understanding someone's viewpoint before challenging it is central to respect. But if the social exchange stops at understanding each other, learning is likely to be limited. Challenge is also needed. For example, when identifying the conditions within schools and particular classrooms that may be limiting professional and student learning, it is crucially important that ideas are put forward in respectful ways, are examined—together with the evidence underpinning them—for their worth, and are rigorously debated.

If the process is disrespectful of individuals, those involved feel blamed and shamed, and learning is stymied. If there is no debate or challenge, then it is likely that only one perception will be taken as valid while others keep alternative views to themselves. A diagram (Figure 2.2) developed by Hopkins, Ainsco, and West (1994) summarises the relationship between trust and challenge and their impact on particular tasks. They argue that moving forward on tasks requires both trust and challenge to be high. Any other combination fails to achieve the aim of building better schools, because either the focus on task accomplishment becomes low, or the focus is high but not supportive so the relationship keeps breaking down. Our observations of many interactions within and between schools show that achieving high trust and challenge is one of the most difficult tasks facing schools' improvement efforts.

Figure 2.2 Levels of trust and challenge, and the relationship to outcomes

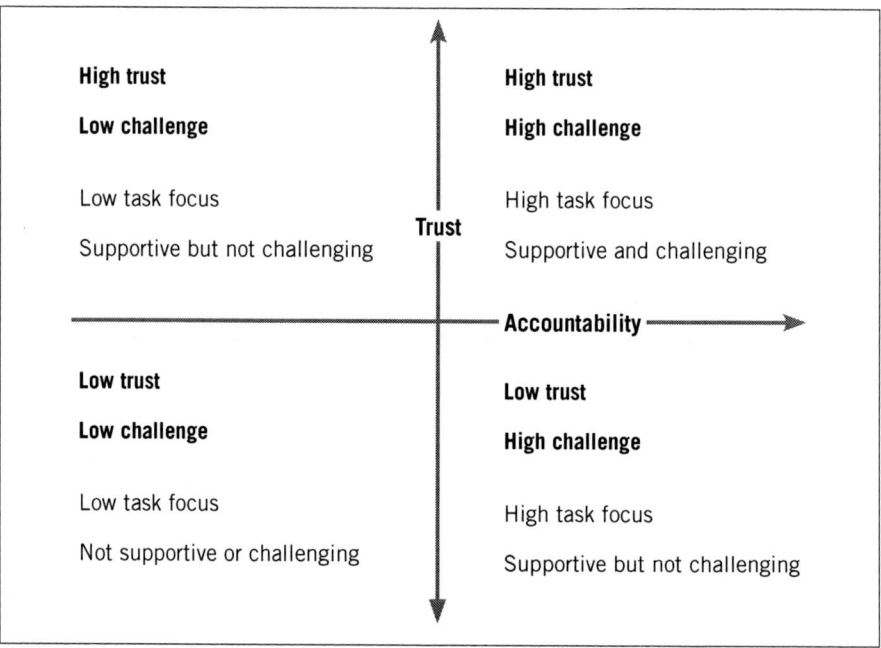

The continuum of development

Instructional, organisational and evaluative capabilities develop over time through multiple cycles of inquiry and knowledge building. They are core capabilities with which to undertake successful inquiry, and are further developed and strengthened through this process. This is why the cycles of inquiry depicted in Figure 2.1 show development and integration of these capabilities over time. The developmental process is not linear but rather progresses in fits and starts, with much revisiting. Those involved learn how to mine the evidence to decide what needs to be focused on, how to differentiate the knowledge and skills likely to have the greatest

It is important to think about where your school fits on each of the dimensions, together with the evidence base underpinning these judgements.

impact from those with less impact and how to judge whether everyone's efforts have been worthwhile.

As we have worked with schools across the country, we have noted how most schools progress towards the development of integrated levels of instructional, organisational and evaluative capability as they work through cycles of inquiry and knowledge building. Through this work we have identified a continuum of progress, from basic to integrated levels of capability (see Table 2.1). We have organised each continuum around the inquiry and knowledge-building cycles illustrated in Figure 1.1. The reason for the use of a continuum for each dimension of the cycle is that we know from research into schooling improvement that optimal models are effective only if those using them can see where their current practice sits, and they have some knowledge of what is needed for improvement. Knowing has a developmental history and requires systems, processes and interpersonal relationships to be built over time.

For this reason we have briefly portrayed typical features of activities in schools according to three points on a continuum: basic, middle/mixed and integrated. In doing so we are not suggesting that development is stage-like or unitary, or that any school would neatly fit any one of the descriptions we have provided. Rather, the descriptions are intended to be illustrative examples, with schools deciding on their approximate or best fit. These judgements may be likened to an "overall judgement", as required by the national standards. How these activity descriptions fit with the different capabilities and relationships described earlier in this chapter are also noted on each continuum in the right-hand column. These descriptions have been formulated for basic and integrated points only on the continuum in order to reduce repetition.

TABLE 2.1 Evidence and inquiry: an illustrative continuum on each dimension of the inquiry and knowledge-building cycle

Dimension 1: Identifying valued outcomes and student learning needs		
	TYPICAL ACTIVITIES	**CAPABILITIES* AND RELATIONSHIPS**
Basic	• Students are routinely assessed using a single externally referenced assessment that is assumed to be assessing the outcomes that are valued and to be appropriate for all contexts. • Analysis allows comparison with other students of the same age, ethnicity and gender, and over time, from the beginning to the end of the year. • School leaders analyse the results. • Student learning needs are identified at a general level (e.g., students are low on reading) and only one area of *The New Zealand Curriculum* (*NZC*) is considered.	**Capabilities** • Low EC: previous routines shape future activities, with the value of outcomes and sources of information assumed. • Low OC: the opportunity is missed to develop shared understanding and responsibility and to utilise wider expertise within staff. • Low IC: unable to delineate the specifics of diagnosis or intervention. **Relationships** Teachers are passive recipients of information.
Middle/ mixed	• Students are routinely assessed using a range of assessments to make an on-balance judgement, but this is not specifically linked to a shared understanding of what outcomes are valued and whether the assessments are appropriate for the context. • Analyses allow comparison with other students of the same age, ethnicity and gender, from the beginning to the end of the year. • Leaders and teachers analyse and discuss the results together, with implications for teaching and learning discussed. • Student learning needs are linked to assessment information, with more specific areas identified (e.g., students are having difficulty with reading comprehension) and areas of *NZC* are considered separately.	
* For capabilities, "IC" refers to instructional capability, "OC" refers to organisational capability and "EC" refers to evaluative capability.		

| Integrated | • A shared understanding of outcomes that are valued is achieved among the whole school community, with a range of assessments used to make an overall teacher judgement that is aligned to these outcomes (including both those that are externally benchmarked and those with specific diagnostic qualities).
• Analyses answer key questions, with particular focuses for information on teaching and learning and patterns of progress within a year and over more than one year.
• Explanations sought for patterns of progress include the whole school community and include conditions over which the school has influence that may be limiting the effectiveness of teaching and learning.
• Student learning needs are identified from a detailed analysis of the assessment information (e.g., students are unable to interpret metaphorical and colloquial uses of language that impede comprehension), with implications for progress across the curriculum considered. | **Capabilities**
High EC: there are multiple sources of evidence and the value of particular outcomes is debated.
IC, OC and EC integrated: assessments are linked to teaching and learning, and a whole curriculum focus is taken. Both instructional and organisational explanations for conditions limiting effectiveness are sought.

Relationships
The whole school community is striving for high trust and high challenge. |

Dimension 2: Identifying professional learning needs: leaders and teachers		
	TYPICAL ACTIVITIES	**CAPABILITIES* AND RELATIONSHIPS**
Basic	• Evidence from student assessments is linked generically to a professional learning focus that is determined for teachers by leaders or professional development providers. • There is anecdotal analysis of teacher knowledge and/or practice, but criteria and evaluation are not co-constructed with teachers. • Leaders organise for the implementation of a generic professional learning plan to support teachers.	**Capabilities** Low IC, OC and EC: there are nonspecific links between assessment, instruction and professional development. **Relationships** There is a high dependence on outside agencies, or uncritical acceptance of internal expertise with low challenge.
Middle/ mixed	• Evidence from student assessments is linked specifically to a professional learning focus, selected by leaders and discussed with teachers. • There is analysis of teacher knowledge and practice in the area of the professional learning focus, with evaluations co-constructed with teachers. • Leader development is identified from effective leadership practice in general, but is not specific to supporting teacher learning in the area of identified need.	
Integrated	• Links analysed between the evidence from student assessment information and evidence of teacher knowledge and practice are specific for each teacher's professional learning focus. • Analysis of teacher knowledge and practice in the area of professional learning focus, with criteria and evaluations, is co-constructed with teachers. • Evidence is also collected on leadership practice with professional learning, focused on what each leader specifically needs to learn and do to professionally support teachers in an area of identified need.	**Capabilities** High IC, OC and EC: there are specific links between evidence of student outcomes, teaching and leadership practice, with priority given to developing adaptive expertise. **Relationships** There is high trust and challenge with external agencies working to scaffold leaders and teachers to use evidence-informed practices.

* For capabilities, "IC" refers to instructional capability, "OC" refers to organisational capability and "EC" refers to evaluative capability.

Dimension 3: Engagement in professional learning to deepen knowledge and refine skills		
	TYPICAL ACTIVITIES	**CAPABILITIES* AND RELATIONSHIPS**
Basic	• The generic knowledge and skills focus of professional learning activities are linked to a generic student learning problem. • Effectiveness is judged by the willingness of teachers to participate. • Professional learning opportunities are externally provided, with leaders keeping in touch (there is no specific professional development for leaders).	**Capabilities** Low IC and OC: the development of adaptive expertise is a low priority. **Relationships** There is high trust and low challenge, with uncritical dependence on external experts.
Middle/ mixed	• A more specific knowledge and skills focus of professional learning is linked to the identified student learning problem. • Effectiveness is judged by teachers' reactions and reported changes to practice. • Professional learning opportunities are led primarily by external providers, with leaders keeping in touch (leader-specific professional learning opportunities are separate from those for the teachers).	
Integrated	• An understanding is developed of how professional learning opportunities need to be consistent with how professionals learn, and research about effective teaching practices is linked to the specifics of a student learning problem. • Effectiveness is judged by the depth of professional learning and changes in classroom practice. • The focus of leadership professional development is to take over from external providers and lead professional learning in the school.	**Capabilities** High IC and OC: opportunities to learn are differentiated for teachers and students depending on their particular needs. **Relationships** The focus is on high trust/challenge and the development of adaptive experts. External agents and leaders are developing interdependence.
* For capabilities, "IC" refers to instructional capability, "OC" refers to organisational capability and "EC" refers to evaluative capability.		

Dimension 4: Engagement of students in new learning experiences		
	TYPICAL ACTIVITIES	**CAPABILITIES* AND RELATIONSHIPS**
Basic	• Effective implementation of new teaching practices is either not checked or is checked for the extent of compliance with specified practices (a checklist approach). • Students' views about learning are not sought.	**Capabilities** Low OC: there is a reliance on voluntary change or compliance. *Relationships* There is either high trust/low challenge when change is voluntary, or low trust/high challenge when compliance is expected.
Middle/mixed	• Effective implementation of new leadership and instructional practices is checked anecdotally; variability is expected but not discussed. • Students' views about learning are collected anecdotally and discussed among staff.	
Integrated	• Effective implementation of new leadership and instructional practices is systematically checked, with variability discussed and addressed by school and relevant experts. • Students' views about learning are systematically sought and acted on.	*Capabilities* High IC, OC and EC: information provides the basis for explanations of outcomes and the development of adaptive expertise. *Relationships* There is high trust/challenge, and the development of organisational and teaching adaptive expertise through interdependence.
* For capabilities, "IC" refers to instructional capability, "OC" refers to organisational capability and "EC" refers to evaluative capability.		

Dimension 5: Assessment of impact and re-engagement in the next cycle		
	TYPICAL ACTIVITIES	CAPABILITIES* AND RELATIONSHIPS
Basic	• Students are reassessed and averages compared with previous averages and national averages for different groups, with no other data monitored systematically to identify possible causes of improvement (or lack of it). • Leaders present data to teachers to discuss and celebrate successes. • Student assessment information is considered anecdotally in the next cycle of assessment and professional learning plan.	**Capabilities** Low OC and EC: student data are unable to be analysed for causal factors and are not linked to ongoing inquiry. **Relationships** There is high trust/low challenge, with an emphasis on success.
Middle/ mixed	• Students are reassessed and averages are compared with previous averages and national averages for different groups, with anecdotal data on teaching practice considered in terms of possible causes of improvement (or lack of it). • Student data are discussed in depth with teachers to understand student successes and areas of ongoing difficulty, but data on teachers are not part of the analysis. • Student assessment information is considered in developing the next cycle of assessment and the professional learning plan.	
* For capabilities, "IC" refers to instructional capability, "OC" refers to organisational capability and "EC" refers to evaluative capability.		

Integrated	• Students are reassessed with information considered in terms of shared understanding of targets and agreed rates of progress towards outcomes that are valued, together with information on leadership and teaching practices, to identify relationships with improvement (or lack of it). • Student data are combined with data on teaching and leadership practices considered part of a formative assessment cycle (short and long term), leading to discussion of possible causal relationships evident in the data and further cycles of inquiry and knowledge building. • Possible unintended consequences are identified. • All information is considered in developing the next cycle of assessment and the professional learning plan to answer the questions, "Where am I going?", "How am I doing?" and "Where to next?"	**Capabilities** High IC, OC and EC: an emphasis is placed on developing adaptive expertise and ongoing inquiry. **Relationships** There is high trust/challenge through close monitoring, and managed interdependence between school personnel and external agents.

Reflection questions

QUESTION 1

Using the descriptions in the framework, decide whether your school is basic, mixed/middle or integrated for each dimension of the inquiry and knowledge-building cycle (see Table 2.1).

a. Dimension 1: Identifying valued outcomes and student learning needs

BASIC	MIDDLE/MIXED	INTEGRATED

b. Dimension 2: Identifying professional learning needs: leaders and teachers

BASIC	MIDDLE/MIXED	INTEGRATED

c. Dimension 3: Engagement in professional learning to deepen knowledge and refine skills

BASIC	MIDDLE/MIXED	INTEGRATED

e. Dimension 5: Assessment of impact and re-engagement in the next cycle

BASIC	MIDDLE/MIXED	INTEGRATED

QUESTION 2

What is the evidence for deciding that the school is basic, mixed/middle or integrated in each of the above dimensions? (Note it for each dimension.)

QUESTION 3

If your school is at the basic or mixed/middle level of the framework, how can you develop school capacity to reach a more integrated level?
What expertise and resources will you need to achieve more integrated practice?

References

Bandura, A. (1995). Exercise of personal and collective self-efficacy in changing societies. In A. Bandura (Ed.), *Self efficacy in changing societies* (pp. 1–45). Cambridge: Cambridge University Press.

Bransford, J., Derry, S., Berliner, D., & Hammerness, K. (2005). Theories of learning and their roles in teaching. In L. Darling-Hammond & J. Bransford (Eds.), *Preparing teachers for a changing world* (pp. 40–87). San Francisco: John Wiley & Sons.

Bryk, A., Sebring, P., Allensworth, E., Luppescu, S., & Eason, J. (2007). *Organising schools for improvement*. Chicago: University of Chicago Press.

Bryk, A. S., Sebring, P. B., Kerbow, D., Rollow, S., & Easton, J. Q. (1998). *Charting Chicago school reform: Democratic localism as a lever for change*. Boulder, CO: Westview Press.

Elmore, R. (2004). *School reform from the inside out: Policy, practice and performance*. Cambridge, MA: Harvard Education Press.

Hattie, J., & Timperley, H. (2007). The power of feedback. *Review of Educational Research, 77*(1), 81–112.

Hopkins D., Ainscow, M., & West, M. (1994). *School improvement in an era of change*. London: Cassell.

Katz, S., Earl, L., & Ben Jafaar, S. (2009). *Building and connecting learning communities: The power of networks in school improvement*. Thousand Oaks, CA: Corwin Press.

Lai, M. K., McNaughton, S., Timperley, H., & Hsiao, S. (2009). Sustaining continued acceleration in reading comprehension achievement following an intervention. *Educational Assessment, Evaluation and Accountability, 21*(1), 81–100. [doi: 10.1007/s11092-009-9071-5.]

March, J. (1996). Exploration and exploitation in organizational learning. In M. Cohen & L. Sproull (Eds.), *Organizational learning* (pp. 101–123). Thousand Oaks, CA: Sage.

McNaughton, S., & Lai, M. (2009). A model of school change for culturally and linguistically diverse students in New Zealand: A summary of evidence from systematic replication. *Teaching Education, 20*(1), 1–21.

Robinson, V., Hōhepa, M., & Lloyd, C. (2009). *School leadership and student outcomes: Identifying what works and why: A best evidence synthesis.* Wellington: Ministry of Education.

PART

TWO

PREPARING FOR CHANGE

CHAPTER THREE

Theories for Improvement and Sustainability[1]

Mei Lai, Helen Timperley and Stuart McNaughton

Everyone has ideas about what to do to become more effective and build better schools. This chapter explains how these ideas can be developed and evaluated so that everyone agrees about how best to improve their practices. When these ideas are coherently linked together they become a theory for improvement. This chapter also identifies some important qualities of these theories to ensure that improvement efforts are sustained over the long term. Evidence is integral to an effective theory for improvement as those involved inquire into the causes of particular problems, seek effective solutions and evaluate their effectiveness.

What is a theory for improvement and why do we need one?

In essence, a theory is just a set of linked ideas to explain something. A theory for improvement is therefore a set of linked ideas about how to improve valued outcomes. Our definition of theory here includes both "formal" theories (e.g., research theories about how to improve reading

> A theory for improvement is a set of linked ideas about how to improve valued outcomes.

---

1   We wish to acknowledge the support received through the Teaching and Learning Research Initiative project on sustainability in the preparation of this chapter.

comprehension) and less formal and tacit theories. An example of a tacit theory is a teacher's ideas during a lesson about how to improve students' meta-cognitive skills. Everyone is a "theorist" in the sense that he or she has a tacit understanding of how to act in particular situations.

A theory for improvement is a powerful way of explaining, evaluating and improving practice. An individual's or a group's theories will guide practices in as much as the theories will result in the individual or group members choosing some practices over others. For example, a school might choose an intervention that focuses on student engagement rather than on classroom instruction because the school considers that improving engagement will result in better student achievement.

It is important to evaluate theories because not all theories will contribute equally to desired outcomes.

Underlying that decision is a theory that (a) students who are engaged will learn and achieve better than students who are less engaged, and (b) intervening in classroom instruction is going to be less effective than fostering student engagement in terms of improving student outcomes. Given that theory, an intervention that focuses on student engagement will be deemed more effective for improving student outcomes than an intervention focused on classroom instruction.

When we explain our theories for improvement to others, we are making our thinking explicit to them (and to ourselves) so that others understand why we think certain practices are more effective than others. Making our theories explicit, together with the evidence underpinning them, is important because it helps us uncover the reasons (and assumptions) we have chosen some practices over others (Robinson & Lai, 2006). When others are explicit about their theories, it helps us examine the reasons and assumptions why they have chosen some practices over others. Uncovering the reasons and assumptions for theories allows us to evaluate the effectiveness of our respective theories, and evaluating theories is fundamental to becoming more effective, because not all theories will contribute equally to desired outcomes. Effective theories demand high levels of organisational, instructional and evaluative capabilities (see Chapter Two), because a range of evidence and information needs to be brought to bear to decide why one theory might be more robust than another.

The following example illustrates how we can explain and examine our theories for improvement in a challenging environment to become more effective. It uses the example of a school where the staff have different theories about the introduction of the national standards.

A school has had many disagreements about the implementation of the national standards. The school is divided into two groups: those who believe it is a terrible idea and those who support the standards. The principal asks each group to explain their theory for supporting or not supporting the standards. The first group's theory is that the standards would be detrimental to student learning and achievement because they would result in narrowing the curriculum. The second group's theory is that having explicit standards would support student learning and achievement because teachers will know exactly what students of a particular age should be achieving and what they need to do next to support students.

As both groups outline their theories they realise that they are basing their views on a set of assumptions. The first group assumes that school leaders will insist that the curriculum focus be narrowed to cover only the standards, and so the standards will automatically be detrimental to student learning. The second group assumes that having explicit knowledge of the standards will automatically lead to improvements in teaching because expected standards of achievement will give teachers greater clarity.

By making their theories explicit, both groups realise two things: everyone shares the common goal of improving student learning. It is not the standards per se that are the problem but rather the assumptions teachers bring to them that make them think in terms of whether they might be positive or negative. When used as evidence for the purpose of enhancing teaching and learning, standards can be effective in supporting student learning but when used for punitive accountability, they can be detrimental to student learning. Thus, the school learns that in order to be effective it needs to focus on using the standards in ways that support student learning and reduce the emphasis on compliance and accountability that could lead to narrow teaching.

What does a theory for improvement look like?

Below is a summary of the components of a theory for improvement. It locates a theory within the process of inquiry that can lead to improved valued student outcomes (Table 3.1). Underpinning this summary is our assumption that effective theories are those that help the school solve the teaching and learning problems it faces. (By "problem" we mean a gap between the desired and existing state of affairs; see Sadler (1989).) The components of the theory need to be based on evidence from your own school (e.g., student achievement data, observations of classroom practice) and research evidence.

Table 3.1 Components of a theory for improvement and their relationship to the inquiry cycle

	Components of a theory for improvement	Inquiry cycle
Linked together	A definition of the problem the theory is designed to address: current understanding of what caused the problem and how the different causes of the problem might interrelate	Defining the problem requires knowing what students' learning strengths and learning needs are, as well as your professional strengths and learning needs (i.e., the first two boxes of the inquiry cycle in Figure 1.1). Standards can be part of the evidence of students' learning needs. The theory for improvement contributes to the inquiry cycle by expanding on how to use the information gathered from the first two boxes in the inquiry cycle to develop an understanding of the problem that schools need to solve.
	Proposed solutions to address directly the causes of the problem, which are understood by all involved	The proposed solutions expand on question two, box two, of the inquiry cycle, "What do we need to learn and do to meet our students' learning needs?", by outlining what is required for a good proposed solution.
	A strong reason for choosing the solutions, including evidence that the solution is going to be effective in addressing the problem	This evidence is brought to bear when deciding what knowledge and skills should be emphasised (box three of the inquiry cycle in Figure 1.1, "Engagement of leaders and teachers in professional learning experiences").
	Interim and long-term desired outcomes, against which progress can be judged, including what counts as success in meeting the targets	The interim and long-term desired outcomes link to the last box in the inquiry cycle, "What has been the impact of our changed actions?", by expanding on how to examine the impact of changed actions. Standards can be seen as part of the desired outcomes.
	Ways to monitor progress towards the targets	Monitoring progress towards targets links to the inquiry cycle boxes on "Engagement of students in new learning experiences" and "What has been the impact of changed actions?" by expanding on how to monitor student learning of new experiences and how to monitor the impact of changed actions. Standards can be seen as a way of supporting teachers to monitor their progress.

Developing and refining a theory for improvement is an integral part of the inquiry cycle. It is an ongoing process that involves identifying and solving problems to achieve the desired student outcomes. This process includes checking whether the nature of the problem has changed as efforts to improve have a positive impact. For example, last year the problem facing a particular school might have been the poor decoding skills of students, but this year the students may have already developed fluent and accurate decoding so the problem has now shifted to vocabulary acquisition. The time frame for developing and refining a theory can occur through an annual review, and could be shorter or longer depending on the nature of the problem and the difficulties experienced in solving it.

The process for developing and refining a theory for improvement is essentially the same across all school contexts, but the specifics of how a theory for improvement is developed could vary. For example, a community with a history of working together, and one that has established relationships of trust and challenge, is likely to engage in a different (and perhaps faster) process for identifying problems compared with a community working together for the first time.

The solution to the problem will also be specific to the context because it will have been designed to meet identified needs. So the content of reading comprehension professional development, for example, will have been tailored to the specific needs of the teachers and students in that school. In other words, the theory for improvement should lead to a solution that is tailored to meet the needs of the local context.

A theory for improvement should include a theory for how to sustain the outcomes that are valued by the school and the community. Sustainability is, in part, a process of organisational learning to improve outcomes already achieved (Lai, McNaughton, Timperley, & Hsiao, 2009). As such, our theory for sustainability is an ongoing process that follows on from initial improvements made. For this reason, sustainability is not something that is planned for after an intervention: it needs to be planned for from early on in the intervention cycles. By this we mean that the school would develop the components of the theory for improvement described in Table 3.1, and then, over time, pinpoint the specific practices that led to the intended valued outcomes. This will help to ensure these practices can be sustained. As a result, a common pattern of initial improvement in valued outcomes which then declines over time can be addressed.

> A theory for improvement should include a theory for sustainability. Sustainability is a process of organisational learning to improve outcomes already achieved.

Here are some things that need to be in place before considering sustaining the work being undertaken:

- There have been verified improvements in student achievement at the desired rate of progress and/or to the desired level over time.
- The instructional and organisational practices known to address the problems have been identified, including any modifications to practices (e.g., how teachers might have adapted practices to their classrooms).
- The processes used to identify and solve problems—and monitor solutions—are known.

We have identified three components that are needed for ongoing sustainability. The first involves developing cycles of inquiry that allow schools to learn using evidence of the effectiveness of their practices, what they need to do next and what they need to stop doing. Part of this process involves developing instructional and organisational capabilities that lead to the teaching and leadership practices and processes that were essential to maintaining and creating ongoing improvement. It is also important to have in place evaluative systems and processes to identify new challenges and how they will be acted on: what is working well and should be retained, what is not and should be examined further to decide what needs to change.

The second component involves embedding practices and processes that are essential to maintaining or improving valued outcomes, and embedding cycles of inquiry in schools' "core business" as part of a coherent instructional programme. By embedding we mean the practices and processes essential to improving valued outcomes and the cycle of inquiry become taken-for-granted features of the school. They become part of the school's norms, structures, practices and culture. Coherence in this context means that schools develop a set of interrelated instructional programmes for students and staff that are guided by a common framework for curriculum, instruction, assessment and learning climate, and that are pursued over a sustained period (Newmann, Smith, Allensworth, & Bryk, 2001).

The third component involves creating interdependence with others. By this we mean developing partnerships with experts within the school (e.g., other teachers) or outside the school (e.g., other schools, researchers, professional developers) to support the school to sustain improvements in student achievement. Interdependence needs to be managed, however. Too much dependence on others can create a cycle of dependency for the school, where the school is overly dependent on others to solve its problems, but with too little external help the school may not have sufficient expertise to address its problems quickly and efficiently.

How do we evaluate a theory for improvement?

We can evaluate and adjust a theory for improvement by checking and monitoring whether:

- the factual claims underpinning the theory are accurate (e.g., is it true that children speak only Samoan at home?)
- the knowledge base for choosing particular theories is adequate (e.g., should we really be following the practices recommended by a milestone report that only reported on teacher satisfaction?)
- the reasoning and subsequent actions result in desired outcomes (e.g., did the professional development raise achievement as intended?)
- the theory for improvement unintentionally creates problems elsewhere (e.g., did the professional development raise achievement in literacy, but unintentionally reduce achievement in numeracy because of reduced class time in numeracy?)
- the theory for improvement is aligned with what we know to be good practice (e.g., is the theory for improvement based on poor practices, such as teaching to the test or cheating?) (Robinson & Lai, 2006).

If, after several cycles of implementing and evaluating the theory for improvement, the problem remains unsolved (e.g., student achievement does not increase as planned), it is important to do something different rather than repeat what has not worked. It is likely that the school will need to bring in external expertise to conduct a detailed problem analysis and/or to design, implement and monitor the solution.

The capabilities needed for a robust theory for improvement

An effective process for developing and monitoring a theory for improvement needs to be both relevant and rigorous (Robinson & Lai, 2006). The process needs to be relevant to key stakeholders to help them solve the problems they are facing, and sufficiently rigorous to provide a trustworthy basis for making decisions about how to improve student outcomes.

Theories for improvement need to be both relevant and rigorous.

Designing and monitoring an effective theory for improvement is the highest level in the developmental continuum, requiring sophisticated instructional, organisational and evaluative capabilities that would be placed at the "integrated" end (see Chapter Two). Designing a theory for improvement requires integrating many different types of knowledge and skills, such as:

- the capability to examine multiple sources of data to identify the specific problems facing the school
- the capability to link achievement patterns to instructional patterns
- strong content and pedagogical content knowledge to know how best to address identified problems
- the capability to collect and analyse evidence to monitor effectiveness
- the capability to bring it all together to be integrated into organisational systems and processes.

The basic or middle/mixed level

The following case study sums up some of the many difficulties schools face when developing a theory for improvement when evaluative capability is still in the lower levels of the developmental continuum (i.e., basic or middle/mixed).

We can look more closely at the capabilities evident in the scenario by using the development continuum. Tables 3.2 and 3.3 show the basic and middle/mixed levels of capability for developing and monitoring a theory for improvement. A more integrated picture is described in a second scenario and in Table 3.4.

We would expect most schools starting to define their theories for improvement to be at the basic level, with uncritical dependence on what the school already knows or on the knowledge of others outside the school. Moving towards a more integrated level should be a priority so that schools can advance towards sustainability. If a school is still operating at the basic level after many years of improvement efforts, it is likely the theory for improvement is flawed and it is unlikely the school will be successful in sustaining effective practices or programmes. Sustainability demands the capability to identify what worked and why, what should be retained and what should be discarded.

> Developing evaluative capability should be a priority for schools so that they can move towards sustainability.

CASE STUDY 3.2

School A is enthusiastic about raising the achievement of its students. The school knows that examining achievement information is important, so it spends months trying to agree on what achievement data to collect, how to collect and moderate the data and how to analyse it. At this stage no one in the school systematically examines what is happening in classrooms, so little is known about the school's teaching practices and how they might relate (or not) to the achievement patterns.

The school organises a few sessions to discuss the achievement data, but in these discussions the focus is on understanding the analysis (e.g., how many students are below the standard) rather than trying to work out what might be causing the problems and how to solve them. The analysis shows that reading comprehension for some subgroups is below the standard.

"So why do you think reading comprehension is low for these groups and what should we do about it?" asks the deputy principal. Everyone voices an opinion based on experience, but no evidence is required about whether the opinions and suggestions are more likely to be successful than what they are doing now. The brainstormed list of what might be causing the low achievement is long, and some teachers start to feel discouraged, partly because they don't have sufficient skills and knowledge to determine if some approaches are likely to be more effective than others.

"So what do we do next to improve reading comprehension?" asks the principal. The staff brainstorm which consultant they might bring in to help them, but do not link their opinions of whom to bring in (and what expertise the consultant might have) with their multiple theories of what caused the problem. Then the staff start debating what they should focus on. The principal believes they should focus on student engagement; one teacher thinks that more explicit teaching of comprehension strategies is required; another feels that parent–school relationships are the key. The meeting reaches an impasse, so the deputy principal offers to collate all the ideas and write what he thinks they need to do next. The document lists five "effective teaching practices" and four strategies for increasing student engagement, which they hope will accomplish the goal of improving reading comprehension. It is unclear how these teaching practices and strategies relate to the reasons for the low reading comprehension and why they might be more effective than what the school is currently doing.

Table 3.2 Basic theory for improvement

Component of the theory for improvement	Typical activities
A definition of the problem the theory is designed to address: current understanding of what caused the problem and how the different causes of the problem might interrelate	The achievement problem is defined in a generic way from a single assessment (e.g., raise student achievement because we are two years behind). Other potentially explanatory data (especially classroom data) are not considered. Causes of the problem, if identified, are seen as primarily external to the school and beyond the school's control, but current understanding is untested.
Proposed solutions to directly address the causes of the problem, which are understood by all involved A strong reason for choosing the solutions, including evidence that the solution is going to be effective to address the problem	Proposed solutions are generic (e.g., improve teaching in reading comprehension) and only implicitly related to the problem. There is little or no discussion to establish a shared understanding of the link between the proposed solutions and cause and the desired outcomes.
Interim and long-term targets and what counts as success	There are generic student achievement targets and/or generic notions of success (e.g., student achievement improves). There is little or no specification of what the school wants to see in the classroom.
Ways to monitor progress towards targets	Data collected to monitor progress are related only to student achievement (there are no classroom practice data, etc. to check implementation).

Theories for improvement change over time, as new information is uncovered to refine the theory or as problems change. For example, new research on how to improve students' writing might change the school's theory, or the existing problem of poor student behaviour is solved, so the school no longer needs to focus on that problem in its theory for improvement. In other words, a theory for improvement needs to be continuously monitored and updated if it is to be effective in achieving the desired outcomes.

Theories for improvement change over time as new information is uncovered or problems change.

The middle/mixed level

At the middle/mixed level of evaluative capability (Table 3.3), the school is likely to take steps to check and monitor continuously the nature of the problem. For example, it may be that there were substantial losses in achievement over the summer holidays (unlike previous years), so teachers may need to plan their programmes to help students accelerate faster to compensate for the loss over summer, or try to offset the decline by involving the community in relevant programmes.

In the middle/mixed level of evaluative capability, dependence on others outside the school is being slowly reduced. For example, monitoring the impact of teaching programmes on valued outcomes should be in the process of being established as the schools' core business. School leaders should be developing school systems and processes that integrate the practices that have worked to improve valued outcomes and incorporating them into the culture of the school (Newmann et al., 2001). Examples of systems include induction, developing appropriate documentation of processes and establishing regular school meetings to carry out tasks.

> School leaders need to develop school systems and processes to integrate the practices that worked to raise achievement and incorporate them into the culture of the school.

The integrated level

At the integrated evaluative capability level, schools see themselves as being responsible for creating continued improvements, although this may mean they seek resources (including time and external expertise) from a variety of sources. For example, school staff could be involved in university courses to develop further expertise, and the school leaders could bring in relevant experts in the field for teacher professional development. In other words, assuming responsibility means developing interdependence with external experts. One aspect of continued interdependence is the need to develop and refine schools' theories of improvement in an ongoing way to become more effective at achieving valued outcomes. External experts can bring new research-based knowledge to this process, but also gain new insight from the schools' knowledge and practices.

Table 3.3 Middle/mixed theory for improvement

Component of the theory for improvement	Typical activities
A definition of the problem the theory is designed to address: current understanding of what caused the problem and how the different causes of the problem might interrelate	The achievement problem is expressed primarily in general ways, using nationally benchmarked assessment. School staff (e.g., teachers) are peripherally involved in the analysis and interpretation. Other relevant data to determine the nature of the problem (e.g., classroom and school data to identify teaching and leadership needs) are informally collected. These data may be used in conjunction with achievement data to determine what might have caused the achievement problem. Both internal and external causes are acknowledged, and the school takes responsibility for the practices it can control. Some current understanding of what might have caused the achievement problem is discussed (including with key stakeholders), but this evaluation is not systematic (e.g., staff have developed a list of "causes" of the achievement problem, but only present evidence for some).
Proposed solutions to directly address the causes of the problem, which are understood by all involved A strong reason for choosing the solutions, including evidence that the solution is going to be effective to address the problem	Proposed solutions are expressed specifically but are focused on classrooms. More explicit links are made between proposed solutions, hypothesised causes and desired outcomes (not necessarily evidence based). There is some discussion of whether there is general agreement on the proposed solutions by key stakeholders.
Interim and long-term targets and what counts as success	Student achievement targets and success criteria are beginning to be differentiated (e.g., different targets for males and females based on achievement data). There is some specification of desired classroom practices.
Ways to monitor progress towards targets	Data are collected to monitor progress in student achievement. Informal school and classroom data are collected. Data collected for monitoring purposes are only implicitly related to the perceived cause of the problem (i.e., it is not always clear why the school is collecting particular types of data to monitor progress). Some data are collected to identify why the implemented solution worked or did not work. Informal observations, such as walkthroughs, may be used to assess implementation.

The following scenario illustrates what developing and monitoring a theory for improvement might look like at an "integrated" level of evaluative capability.

CASE STUDY 3.3

School B wants to improve what it is doing to accelerate student achievement in reading comprehension. The school decides to collect data on students' abilities using achievement data and observations of students during normal classroom practices to understand students' learning needs. The school also collects data using observations of teachers' classroom practices and of leaders facilitating staff meetings to identify the leaders' and teachers' professional learning needs. The school has some emerging theories about the specific classroom and leadership practices that are associated with the achievement patterns. The school knows that it has some capacity to draw the links between the practices and the achievement patterns, and that through partnership with external experts the links could be made more precisely. So they engage the services of a research development team to help them make those links.

Analysis of the achievement data indicates several specific problems, such as the need to accelerate the achievement of students at the average reading levels, who appear to be making little gain yearly, and addressing the issue of extremely low vocabulary scores of male students. The process of linking the achievement patterns to the classroom and leadership practices pinpoints specific practices that could be contributing to the achievement problems listed, such as an overemphasis on working with students at the lower reading levels.

Separate solutions to address the different student learning needs are developed based on the research development team's previous interventions, which have successfully addressed these student learning needs. Separate targets for each problem are developed, and the evidence collected is used to create specific, yet achievable, targets.

The school develops plans systematically to monitor any improvements in achievement and improvements in teaching and leadership practices. The school examines achievement data at least twice a year using standardised tests, and throughout the year using regular observations of student learning in classrooms. They examine improvements in teaching and leadership practices through a series of recorded observations of classroom and management practices. The plans are integrated into the school's core business so that they are not seen as an "add on".

Discussions are held with key stakeholders (e.g., teachers, community) about the problems and their solutions, and how to monitor them. Where there are disagreements, a process is established to resolve them by examining the evidence for the differing views. The process is used to finalise the school's plan for how to solve the achievement problem.

Table 3.4 Integrated theory for improvement

Component of the theory for improvement	Typical activities
A definition of the problem the theory is designed to address: current understanding of what caused the problem and how the different causes of the problem might interrelate	The assessment selected includes both nationally normed assessment (plus others), and allows for the construction of differentiated profiles of achievement. A range of explanatory factors (including specific classroom practices) is considered and tested systematically. The school works in partnership with stakeholders to address the causes of the problem. Interrelationships between likely causal aspects of the problems are identified. Understanding of the achievement problem and its possible causes is open to evidence-based critique by a range of key stakeholders. A process is established to resolve any disagreements by examining the evidence for the differing views.
Proposed solutions to address directly the causes of the problem, which are understood by all involved Strong reason for choosing the solutions, including evidence that the solution is going to be effective to address the problem	Proposed solutions are specific to the causes of the problem (including examining leadership as well as teaching practices). There is: • alignment of cause, solution and outcome • systematic establishing of whether the proposed solutions are agreed to by key stakeholders. Selection of the solution is evidence-informed, linked to outcomes and explicitly articulated.
Interim and long-term targets and what counts as success	Student achievement targets are differentiated and based on evidence. Specifications for classroom and school practices are based on evidence.
Ways to monitor progress towards targets	Data are collected to monitor progress in student achievement, led primarily by the school. Systematic school, leadership and classroom data related to the causes of the problem are collected to monitor impact. Monitoring processes are embedded into the school's core business and can be used to identify new challenges and problems when they arise.

Table 3.4 shows the details of the activities at the integrated level of the evaluative capability for developing and monitoring a theory for improvement. At the integrated evaluative capability level, the processes and tasks that were essential to maintaining and creating ongoing improvement are now fully embedded in the school's "core business" as part of a coherent instructional programme. A cycle of refining the theory for improvement is in place to identify new challenges and how they will be acted on. The school has established a vehicle—such as professional learning communities—to access and test knowledge systematically the school needs in order to continue improving outcomes. As such, the school has developed a process for ongoing sustainability.

Reflection questions

QUESTION 1

Using the continuum, decide whether your school is basic, mixed/middle or integrated for the following components of the theory for improvement:

a. A definition of the problem the theory is designed to address: current understanding of what caused the problem and how the different causes of the problem might interrelate

BASIC	MIDDLE/MIXED	INTEGRATED

b. Proposed solutions to address directly the causes of the problem, which are understood by all involved:
strong reason for choosing the solutions, including evidence that the solution is going to be effective to address the problem

BASIC	MIDDLE/MIXED	INTEGRATED

c. Interim and long-term targets against which progress can be judged, including what counts as success in meeting the targets

BASIC	MIDDLE/MIXED	INTEGRATED

d. Ways to monitor progress towards the targets

BASIC	MIDDLE/MIXED	INTEGRATED

QUESTION 2

What is the evidence for deciding that your school is basic, mixed/middle or integrated for those components?

BASIC	MIDDLE/MIXED	INTEGRATED

QUESTION 3

Do different people in your school disagree with where you have placed the school on the continuum?

a. What evidence do they have for disagreeing with you?

b. Whose evidence is stronger: yours or theirs?

BASIC	MIDDLE/MIXED	INTEGRATED

QUESTION 4

If your school is at the basic or mixed/middle levels of the continuum, how can you develop school capacity to reach an integrated level? What expertise and resources will you need to reach an integrated level?

BASIC	MIDDLE/MIXED	INTEGRATED

References

Lai, M. K., McNaughton, S., Timperley, H., & Hsiao, S. (2009). Sustaining continued acceleration in reading comprehension achievement following an intervention. *Educational Assessment, Evaluation and Accountability, 21*(1), 81–100.

Newmann, F. M., Smith, B. A., Allensworth, E., & Bryk, T. (2001). Instructional program coherence: What it is and why it should guide school improvement policy. *Educational Evaluation and Policy Analysis, 23*(4), 297–321.

Robinson, V. M. J., & Lai, M. K. (2006). *Practitioner research for educators: A guide to improving classrooms and schools.* Thousand Oaks, CA: Corwin Press.

Sadler, D. R. (1989). Formative assessment and the design of instructional systems. *Instructional Science, 18,* 119–144.

CHAPTER FOUR

Changing Tack: Talking About Change Knowledge for Professional Learning

Deidre Le Fevre

This chapter considers change. Inquiry is empty without the aim of improvement and change. To change tack literally means to start using a different method for dealing with a situation, especially in the way you communicate. If we want to improve learning in order to build better schools, there needs to be a change in how people "talk about change knowledge" (TACK). "Change knowledge" comprises understanding about the processes of change.

Fundamentally, there needs to be more talk about both the processes and substantial content of change that people engage in, because change is such a complex and difficult process. Talking about change has the potential to empower people to work with the challenges inherent in change and help them gain a stronger meta-cognitive awareness of these processes. In order to make these processes explicit, changing TACK might involve considerably more talk about prioritising change, expectations for change, the challenges of change and evaluating change outcomes.

If educational leaders, professional developers and teachers do not have an understanding of the opportunities and challenges inherent in processes of change (change knowledge), then it becomes more difficult to engage in inquiry and use evidence to bring about effective, sustainable change that improves outcomes for students. While inquiry for improvement involves change, change itself as a process needs careful consideration. Talk helps.

> When building better schools, everyone needs to have a sound understanding of the processes of change.

This chapter takes a new perspective to help schools think about engaging in effective change. It aims to provoke discussion among practitioners about developing the skills and understanding to engage in, and talk about, change processes that emanate from evidence-informed inquiry and that have effective outcomes for students. The processes of change discussed in this chapter are applicable across different contexts of educational change, although the specific context discussed here concerns initiatives for professional learning.

The context for talk about change needs to be systemic and should include educational leaders, professional developers, classroom teachers and students, where appropriate. It is recommended that all those involved in building better schools talk about processes of change. This talk should be embedded in everyday actions—a systemic, shared and embedded understanding of the processes inherent in bringing about change to improve outcomes for students. This chapter focuses on the importance of talking about change and provides some examples of a continuum of effective approaches to change in relation to professional learning.

Talking about change requires a different focus for inquiry and additional forms of evidence from those discussed so far in this book. In this chapter, inquiry focuses on the impact of change on teachers and school leaders, and needs to be supported by evidence of this impact. The questions to be answered by this different focus might include:

- Are the changes proposed making sense to those expected to implement them?
- Are sufficient time and resources available for effective change to occur?
- Are the expectations for change realistic?
- Do the relationships among those involved encourage risk taking?

Why talk about change?

Change involves significant and complex issues at the individual, organisational and systemic levels. At times it can feel as if change is being imposed or demanded, and a school may not see the need for the requested or mandated change (such as the introduction of national standards), or have the necessary resources to implement the change successfully. Proposed change might be in conflict with existing activities and philosophies. On the other hand, proposed changes might be "coming down the line", and a school recognises the importance of taking on these new ways of thinking and acting, although it does not know where to begin. Whatever the situation, it is important that leaders, professional developers and teachers are informed and empowered to make decisions regarding change that make sense for their students, staff, school and communities. Four suggested dimensions (see Figure 4.1) for talking about change are discussed, with the goal of informing and empowering leaders, teachers and professional developers involved in making schools more effective places for all learners. These dimensions are:

Change is a central and complex feature of building better schools.

- identifying priorities
- holding high expectations
- communicating challenges
- evaluating outcomes.

We can't improve student learning outcomes by continuing to do the same thing.

Each of these dimensions is considered in turn.

Figure 4.1 Embedding the process of change in professional learning

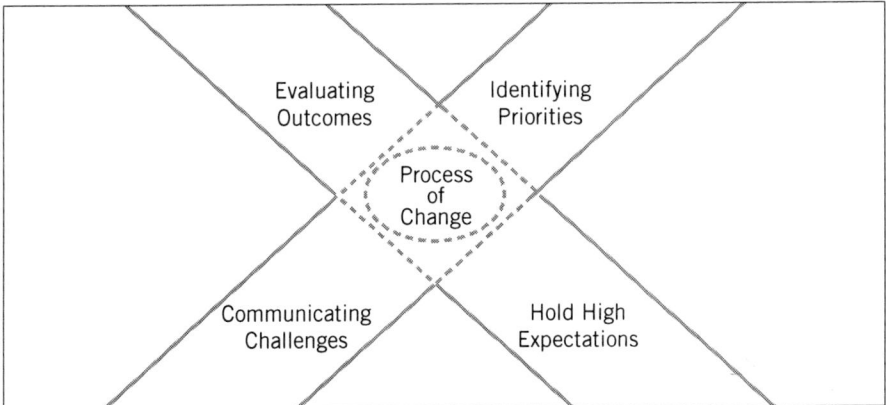

73

Identifying priorities

Change is an important aspect of the life of schools. However, change in itself is not inherently positive and can lead to negative outcomes. Not all change is good, and not all processes of change are desirable. Educational change that results in positive outcomes for student learning and creates schools that are supportive environments to work in is desirable. This does not just happen, and it is important to consider carefully the way we talk about change. First, we may need to prioritise change as a fundamental component of effective schools. This includes two aspects: prioritising change, in terms of making it a central aspect of the work of building better schools, and prioritising what specific changes to implement.

Specific initiatives should be selectively prioritised, with the goal of achieving overarching coherence.

Prioritising change as a central aspect of effective schools means keeping the intention to change teaching and leadership practices constantly on the radar screen. As mentioned in the previous chapter, theories for improvement are inevitably modified over time: they change as new evidence comes to hand. This goal of changing practices demands that leaders take a key role in maintaining coherence between short-, medium- and long-term goals when prioritising specific change initiatives. Prioritising *what* to change demands that leaders and teachers make conscious and transparent decisions about what needs to change by taking a big-picture lens and looking systemically at:

- What is currently happening in this school?
- What does it make sense to maintain?
- What needs to change?
- How much change is too much?

Educational leaders have an important role as change agents within their organisations, and this role includes the task of setting directions for change and prioritising change initiatives. Part of this task requires identifying initiatives that need to be cut or postponed to enable sufficient attention and strategic resourcing to be given to prioritised projects (Robinson, Lloyd, & Rowe, 2008).

Identifying priorities for change requires an understanding of, and information about, what is likely to "work". It is difficult to set priorities if you don't know what to prioritise. A good place to start is to search for evidence of proven, effective practices that have worked in similar contexts. An important aspect of prioritising change is the task of navigating existing options and identifying new professional learning opportunities that create coherence across initiatives and between student and teacher learning needs. This coherence, or alignment, is important for both student and teacher learning needs. It is also important in terms of not having different initiatives for professional learning occurring simultaneously, which can result in multiple goals for teacher learning being pursued at the expense of enabling deep learning to occur in a connected and focused way. Instead, initiatives for staff involvement need to be selected on the basis of evidence of teacher learning needs that have the potential to affect identified and prioritised student learning needs. It is also important that prioritised approaches are aligned in philosophy and pedagogy, because the co-existence of conflicting approaches can cause difficulties and has been demonstrated to have a lower impact on student achievement than more coherent approaches (Bryk, Sebring, Kerbow, Rollow, & Easton, 1998).

Throughout this chapter, examples are provided of a continuum representing different levels of engagement in effective change processes (see Table 4.1). Obviously, because processes of change are so complex, any one school is unlikely to be placed definitively in any single "box". Rather, the examples should be viewed as a guide to some of the perspectives and actions one might expect to find at these different levels. Two case studies of schools engaged in professional learning, representing a prebasic to basic level of engagement and a more integrated level across all dimensions, are used to illustrate the issues.

The idea of coherence is important in prioritising professional learning initiatives and is a key component of organisational capability. When energies are directed towards multiple, sometimes conflicting, initiatives that are not part of an overall coherent plan, then achieving effective change that ultimately improves learning for students is unlikely to be successful. Changes in teaching practices that have the capacity to improve outcomes for students are more likely to occur when there is an overarching plan for both student and teacher learning that is connected, focused and reasonable in scope (O'Connell, 2009).

There is a tendency for schools to engage with multiple and sometimes conflicting professional learning initiatives. At best, engagement with multiple initiatives can be a drain on time and resources without any single initiative being given sufficient attention. At worst, engagement in multiple initiatives can result in a school experiencing quite different and conflicting philosophical and pedagogical approaches. An example of the latter is described in Case study 4.1.

Table 4.1 Continuum of capability: Identifying priorities

	Basic	Mixed	Integrated
Making change central to the work of improving schools	No expectations of change are communicated. Professional learning opportunities are designed primarily on the basis of teacher interests and the expertise of available professional developers.	The goal of changing teaching practices is explicitly communicated in professional learning initiatives, but professional development often occurs without a focus on why and how to change actual practice.	There is a shared understanding that changes in practice are needed, and why. Decisions about professional learning are based on the ongoing identification of specific student learning needs that demand changes in teaching practice.
Prioritising what specific changes to implement	Several professional learning initiatives with varying focuses are undertaken, either simultaneously or in quick succession. Resources are thinly spread across a broad range of initiatives that lack a clear alignment. There is a sense of upheaval evident in relation to the amount of change targeted.	There is engagement in several professional learning initiatives, with some degree of alignment across goals. There remains a tendency to continually take on new initiatives.	There is engagement with specific selected initiatives that have coherence in terms of overarching goals and alignment with medium/long-term prioritised teacher, leader and student learning needs. Resources are sufficient to enable full engagement with selected initiatives and to support sustainability of learning/change.

A professional developer has been working on reading comprehension in a school for 12 months. During her time there she has found that the same staff are simultaneously undertaking professional development with another provider on writing that is at odds with some of the things she herself is trying to promote. This is creating tension, and teachers in the school are not sure what practices to implement. The existence of concurrent and contradictory literacy teaching strategies based on different theoretical rationales is inhibiting teachers from making effective changes to their teaching practices.

Engagement with several different professional development initiatives at any one time can also be problematic in terms of allocating the necessary resources and engaging adequate attention to ensure their effective implementation. Perhaps even more problematic in terms of teachers', leaders' and, ultimately, students' experiences is the confusion of conflicting ideologies between different initiatives that lack coherence and close alignment of purpose. Sometimes it is a case of "less is more" when prioritising professional learning initiatives that will enable deep learning and ultimately result in effective and sustainable change.

Case study 4.2 represents what an integrated level of capability might look like in terms of identifying priorities.

CASE STUDY 4.2

A school is invited to participate in a new professional development writing contract. Student data show that, overall, students are making gains in reading comprehension (their current focus), though they still have some further gains to make. A closer examination of the data indicates, however, that students who are English-language learners have not made the expected levels of progress. The leadership team decides to continue their work on reading comprehension and to work with the provider of writing professional development to ensure the writing development work builds on the work undertaken in reading comprehension to develop better reading–writing links for the English-language learners. They negotiate this specific focus on the needs of the English-language learners in order to create a coherent professional and student learning plan.

Holding high expectations

Effective schools need professional developers and leaders who hold expectations that teachers can and will change how they think and what they do. For a long time now teacher-expectation research (e.g., Good, 1987) has highlighted the significant effect these expectations have on student performance, and the predominant view is that it is important to hold

It is important to hold high expectations of teachers' capability to change.

77

high expectations of students. A parallel notion would suggest it is important that professional developers and leaders hold high expectations of teachers' capacity to change. Teachers deserve the same respect and high expectations of their capabilities to become adaptive experts. The continuum below illustrates what might characterise a school at different levels in terms of expectations of the teachers.

Table 4.2 Continuum of capability: Holding high expectations

	Basic	Mixed	Integrated
Holding high expectations of capability for teachers to change	Talk by professional developers and leaders indicates that only some teachers are expected to change their practice.	High expectations of capability to change practices are held for most staff.	Inclusive and ongoing talk about expected changes to classroom practice is a systemic part of professional learning for all teachers. High expectations of teachers' capability to change and adapt are held by professional developers and leaders.

For change to be integral to improving schools, it is helpful to have clear and explicit expectations that leaders and teachers can and will change their teaching practices. This usually involves making changes to the way they think.

Case study 4.3 illustrates a situation in which there is no, or only limited, explicit mention of expected changes to be made to teaching practices. This expectation is not held by leadership in the school, by the professional developer or by the teachers themselves. In other words, there is no, or limited, accountability at any level for classroom teaching practices to actually change as a result of professional learning. Not only is there an absence of explicit expectations of change, but the message is communicated that it is expected that several people will not change. In contrast, Case study 4.4 represents a more integrated level of capability.

CASE STUDY 4.3

The identified need of the students is an improvement in reading comprehension. There has been much discussion about effective teaching strategies for improving student comprehension, but there has not been any explicit mention made of the expectation that teachers will use, or at least try, these strategies in their classrooms. When interviewed, a professional developer says, "There is no expectation of teachers that having sat there and listened and discussed, they are going to go and try something different in the classroom." Senior management have been overheard to say that they don't expect several of the teachers to take much notice of the suggested strategies, and that they will probably continue teaching the same way as they have for several years now, although others will likely benefit.

CASE STUDY 4.4

The professional developer (who is external to the school) spends time in classrooms observing literacy teaching that focuses on reading comprehension and reading–writing links. In most cases the teachers are willing to have her in their classroom and engage openly in the discussion following the classroom observation. However, a couple of teachers have refused to have the professional developer in their classroom and have said they are not changing the way they do things. Because data from their classes indicate students are struggling with comprehension, the professional developer and school principal persist in developing a relationship with the teachers and in discussing the need to try different strategies in their classrooms. The professional developer offers a compromise: to teach the class herself while the classroom teacher observes and the principal organises release time for the teachers to discuss what happened. This is seen as a somewhat less threatening way to begin engaging teachers. The expectation, however, is that it will be the turn of the teacher to be observed in the future.

This problem of limited expectations for change can be systemic. While it is important to hold higher and clearer expectations of the capacity of teachers to change and adapt, these expectations need to be realistic within the context of teachers' work. Change is challenging on many levels, and so it is important that high expectations for change exist within an environment in which the reasoning for the proposed changes is made transparent and is linked to relevant student learning needs. It is also important that this happens within a supportive environment in which the challenges faced are discussed and worked through in a way that supports teachers, both personally and professionally.

Communicating challenges

Obviously it is not sufficient to hold high expectations of teachers to change. Teachers also need to be actively supported to change. An important element of this support is talk about the challenges inherent in the processes of change. Three challenges of change are:

- addressing the enactment gap
- supporting risk taking
- building relational trust.

Meeting these challenges requires inquiry into the evidence related to teaching practice, teacher beliefs and the levels of trust among teachers and with their leaders.

The challenge of addressing the enactment gap

One challenge of educational change is the problem of the enactment gap (Schon, 1983). There is a major difference between knowing *why* and knowing *how*.

> Knowing *why* demands different skills and understanding to knowing *how*.

Professional learning opportunities might succeed in helping people gain new understanding and theories, but there often remains a gap between what teachers gain in terms of new understanding about classroom practices and what they actually do. Effective change requires that professional developers and leaders, alongside teachers, make visible the difference between knowing *why* and knowing *how* in order to support the enactment of desired changes. Addressing the enactment gap includes having the capacity to identify clearly the difference between knowing what practices make sense and knowing to what degree one is actually engaged in those practices. It involves undertaking strategies to move from predominantly knowing about effective classroom practices to engaging in them on an ongoing basis.

Table 4.3 Continuum of capability: Challenges of change

	Basic	Mixed	Integrated
Addressing the enactment gap	Professional learning involves talk about what to change and why. However, limited connections are made with how to enact change in practice and the challenges therein.	There is some identification of gaps between what is known and what is enacted in terms of prioritised changes to practice.	There is ongoing identification of gaps between knowledge of why/how to change practice and current capacity to actually change practice. Support is provided to continue closing this gap.

There appear to be two types of enactment gap challenges. In some circumstances teachers have professional learning experiences that show them how to change their practice, but the necessary reasoning and theoretical understanding regarding why they should change are not provided. In other situations teachers feel that they have gained in-depth theoretical understanding of *why* they should do things differently but do not know *how* they might actually go about it in their own classrooms and are illustrated in Case studies 4.5 and 4.6. Both scenarios pose a challenge to all involved.

CASE STUDY 4.5

The teachers say they have a good understanding of the reasoning for a proposed new strategy for teaching writing. They have spent a lot of time looking at student writing samples and have read several articles about the suggested teaching strategy in their professional development work. They agree in principle with the need to change the way they are teaching writing. The problem they each communicate privately with one another is that while they see a need to change, they do not yet understand how to go about actually doing this with their students. The private nature of this communication means the problem does not surface in ways that allow it to be addressed.

Professional developers and leaders have an important role in working to close the enactment gap. Providing professional development opportunities that combine the chance to come to grips with both why a suggested practice matters and how to implement it (as illustrated in Case study 4.6) is crucial if effective change is to be sustained.

CASE STUDY 4.6

The teachers have a good understanding of the reasoning for a proposed new strategy for teaching writing and how it connects with reading comprehension, particularly for English-language learners. They are both confident and competent implementing it in practice. Throughout their professional development these teachers have been supported to make connections between theory and practice. For example, they have discussed their own theories of why the strategy may and may not be effective and compared these with indications from the research. They have viewed video records of the strategy being used with other students and have identified the potential challenges of doing so before implementing it in their own classrooms.

The challenge of supporting risk taking

Bringing about effective change involves risk taking. Teachers are in the position of needing to take on new practices, and leaders must commit substantial effort to an uncertain process of change. From this perspective, change involves

> Change is uncertain and requires supported risk taking.

a degree of risk for all involved. In addition, the work of improving schools often comes under considerable external scrutiny (Bryk & Schneider, 2002), so there is often a public side to risk taking. Processes of change involve inherent risk that is rarely discussed upfront due to, for example, fear of inadequacy or failure (see Case study 4.7). A willingness to take risks is crucial to innovation and change, and more talk about what this involves is important to support teachers and leaders alike.

Table 4.4 Continuum of capability: Supporting risk taking

	Basic	Mixed	Integrated
Supporting risk taking	There is a tendency to try to avoid risk and to make "safe" changes that are minimal in scale and impact.	It is accepted that change involves risk taking, but this is not yet linked to problem solving in relation to these risks. "We all make mistakes," but don't necessarily learn from them.	There is understanding that all learning involves risk taking and working with uncertainty. Ongoing learning through risk taking is framed within a problem-solving/ learning perspective.

Teachers in the school undertaking professional development in reading comprehension are reluctant to change their known and familiar ways of teaching. They are afraid of making major changes to their practice because of the public nature of their work and an underlying fear that it might not go well. A teacher says, "When you try something new and mess up, everyone will know about it." For these teachers it feels safer to stay with the known and familiar, or make minor changes to their practice, than to undertake substantial change.

Risk taking is affected by the extent to which schooling and what goes on in the classroom is deprivatised. There may be fear of the very public nature of potential failure. The combination of a normative view of the need to take risks, juxtaposed alongside the anxiety of messing up, suggests that talking about the challenge of risk taking in educational change is an important aspect of effecting educational change. Acknowledgement of the circumstances that create a perception of risk for people is important. Also important are actions that serve to mitigate the degree of actual risk. Case study 4.8 represents a more integrated level of engagement in risk taking.

CASE STUDY 4.8

Even though the teachers have talked about implementation and watched videos of practice, they are still concerned about changing from their known and familiar ways of teaching. The principal and senior leadership team are aware of this underlying fear and talk with teachers individually to identify their different worries. These talks bring to light a number of different concerns, so the principal dedicates a series of staff meetings to talking about the uncertain nature of teaching, sharing his own concerns regarding feeling vulnerable as a leader and the public nature of his work, and brainstorming with staff some possible things the school can do to make it "safer" to try new strategies in the classroom.

Considering where a school might sit on a continuum of supporting risk taking is in itself challenging. Perhaps the key idea is that inherent in change is a degree of uncertainty and risk. Avoiding this risk is likely to limit possibilities for substantial change. At the other end of the continuum is an environment that supports people in taking risks. This support recognises that change involves situations of possible failure and is not punitive in these situations, but instead uses them to problem solve how things might be understood and undertaken differently. Thus, by engaging in the cycle of inquiry (Figure 1.1), supported risk taking is more likely to lead to lasting and effective change. For educational change to be effective it is helpful to talk about the importance of risk taking within an organisational environment of high mutual support and relational trust (Bryk & Schneider, 2002).

The challenge of building relational trust

Building trust among teachers, leaders and professional developers is essential to the creation of an environment in which people are willing to take risks. Bryk and Schneider (2002) identify several qualities of relational trust. These include the importance of treating others with respect, sharing in the performance of a task and having high levels of personal integrity. Their research reveals that the extent of trust among leaders and teachers in a school influences how effective the school is for students. They argue that the presence of high levels of relational trust moderates the sense of uncertainty and vulnerability felt by teachers engaged in educational change. Currently there appear to be pockets of strong relational trust within New Zealand schools, but also numerous gaps where a lack of trust might better describe the culture. Case study 4.9 describes a situation where building trust is impeded.

> Strong relationships built on trust are essential.

Table 4.5 Continuum of capability: Building relational trust

	Basic	Mixed	Integrated
Building relational trust	Collegial conversations are a part of professional learning, but these usually centre on straightforward issues, with an avoidance of tough issues.	Pockets of staff have created safe environments in which to discuss tough issues.	Throughout the school, collegial and challenging conversations are typical of professional learning. Professional developers, teachers and leaders generally feel safe and supported to challenge and discuss tough issues with each other.

CASE STUDY 4.9

In addition to the reading comprehension professional developer, who has been with the school for just over a year, several professional development providers are working either concurrently or in quick succession, and these people do not have the opportunity to work with staff over a sustained period of time. This situation is resulting in a lack of continuity in interchanges between professional developers, leaders and teachers, which is making it difficult to build and maintain adequate levels of relational trust for everyone involved. The reading comprehension professional developer says, "Teachers avoid talking about the tough issues during professional development sessions and do not tend to reveal what they are struggling with because we don't have a relationship with them."

Where professional development enables teachers and leaders to work on initiatives over a sustained period of time, and to build relationships among each other and with professional developers, there is more likely to be a context in which meaningful conversations about tough issues can occur.

Talking about and engaging in educational change requires having sufficient relational trust to be able to engage in difficult conversations about tough issues. It is important for leaders and teachers to take stock of the evidence about the quality of their conversations, because there is a difference between congenial and critical conversations. Where relational trust is low, the nature of conversations might appear congenial on the surface, but significant problems and challenges tend to be avoided. On the other hand, where relational trust is high, it is safe to talk about the tough issues and to debate issues of importance. Effective educational change requires relational trust in order to reduce professionals' sense of vulnerability, facilitate public problem solving, support shared values and goals and create commitment to improving schools (Bryk & Schneider, 2002). Case study 4.10 presents a situation illustrating an integrated level of capability.

In addition to the reading comprehension professional developer, who has been with the school for just over a year, the specialist in developing reading–writing links has also worked with the teachers over the year, but contact was less frequent. The leadership team was aware of the importance of integrating the key messages from these two viewpoints and that respectful and trusting relationships needed to be built with both, so that teachers could discuss the hard stuff of teaching openly and honestly. The professional developer responsible for reading comprehension took the lead role and the leadership team decided she would continue to work with the staff on the long-term plan for at least another year. In order to check their perception that most teachers now felt safe, in sessions facilitated by the professional developer, publicly discussing the struggles they face, they undertook an anonymous survey on the perceived levels of trust and safety among the staff. Although these appeared to be relatively high, few sought the professional developer's support one-on-one to discuss problems of practice.

Evaluating outcomes

The evaluation of change can be thought about in relation to two main tasks: evaluating the processes of change, and evaluating the desired outcomes of change. Each demands different forms of evidence. It is often evidence of outcomes that is given priority, while evidence of processes is neglected. Yet good outcomes are unlikely to be realised if there are poor processes.

Evaluating the process of change requires, first of all, that teachers, leaders and professional developers become aware of the processes they engage in (for example, the presence of the challenges mentioned in this chapter), with the intention of identifying both the practices to continue and the issues that need support and attention.

> Everyone needs to be involved in checking "How are we going?"

Becoming aware that there is such a thing as knowledge about the change process, and then collecting evidence to evaluate how you are doing in talking about and using this knowledge, can help the evaluation process. Questions a school leader might ask, for example, are "On what basis have we made decisions regarding the professional learning to target for staff?" (identifying priorities) or, "What do teachers perceive to be the major risks involved in changing their practice and what have we set up to mitigate these?" (identifying challenges, risk taking).

Evaluating the desired outcomes of change requires a clear focus on what practices are expected to change and evidence of whether or not they have in fact changed. This includes identifying what effect these changes have had on student learning outcomes. This is a challenging but necessary task to undertake. It is challenging because the link between what teachers learn, how they change what happens in the classroom and, subsequently, what this means for student experience and learning in the classroom involves a complex web of actions and beliefs.

Table 4.6 Continuum of capability: Evaluating outcomes

	Basic	Mixed	Integrated
Evaluating the processes of change	Some discussion of challenges faced are informally shared, but there is limited opportunity taken to problem solve.	Explicit summative discussion of the impact of processes of change happens, but this is not yet embedded as an ongoing discussion within professional learning.	Professional learning includes ongoing and explicit discussion of the challenges faced. Ongoing problem solving of possible ways to address challenges is built into professional learning opportunities.
Evaluating the degree to which desired outcomes of change are achieved	Professional learning opportunities are prioritised and evaluated on the basis of teacher satisfaction, with limited attention paid to actual changes (or lack of changes) in teaching practices.	The impact of professional learning on teaching practice is investigated. However, the link between changed teaching practices and student learning outcomes is not investigated.	Ongoing inquiry into the impact of change (or lack of change) in practice on student learning informs subsequent decision making regarding professional learning priorities. There is ongoing engagement with the cycle of inquiry.

CASE STUDY 4.11

At the end of the second term the senior management team compiles a report about the professional development in literacy undertaken over the past 18 months. Every teacher who has participated is given a questionnaire to assess the outcomes and degree of satisfaction with the professional development provided. A couple of teachers write about the impact of the professional development on their classroom practice, a couple mention some new piece of information they learnt, but most discuss their degree of engagement with the actual sessions. No evidence is collected regarding changes to classroom practices or student learning outcomes, or the effectiveness of the change process.

This case study represents a pre-basic to basic engagement in evaluating process and the outcomes of the professional learning initiatives. It would be fair to say that evaluating the degree to which desired outcomes of change are achieved is a challenge in itself. However, if professional learning is in the service of student learning (Elmore, 2004), then it is important that the outcomes of professional learning are examined in terms of outcomes for students. A focused evaluation that includes a range of data sources (as illustrated in case study 4.12), and evidence of effective processes, illustrates a more integrated level of competence.

CASE STUDY 4.12

At the end of the second term the senior management team compiles a report about the professional development in literacy undertaken over the past 18 months. They tap a range of different data sources. For example, they undertake observations of classrooms, collect a sample of student work from teachers and provide teachers with a brief questionnaire, in which they are invited to self-assess (and provide evidence of this assessment) the extent to which they have implemented new teaching strategies in their classroom and the reasons they have or have not done so. Teachers have the opportunity to communicate both supporting and constraining factors on successful implementation and the processes that have helped or hindered them. All the evidence is considered, and a draft report is shared with the teachers to gain input and plan future action.

Conclusions

Changing tack involves changing the way we "talk about change knowledge". Specifically, it is important to inquire into and talk about the work of identifying priorities, holding high expectations and the challenges of change, and using evidence to evaluate outcomes.

Talk about change needs to be undertaken at a systemic level. Unless all the key players involved in implementing change are engaged in talk about priorities, challenges, expectations and outcomes of change, and gather the relevant evidence, improvement is likely to be piecemeal and unsustainable. Talking about change is a critical role for leaders, professional developers and teachers engaged in processes of change. For example, in the case of risk taking, a school leader might acknowledge to staff that making a change involves taking risks and that he/she will support teachers through the uncertainty and fear of failure inherent in this. For the professional developer it might require creating a safe professional space in which teachers can problem solve their failures, while for classroom teachers it might involve identifying what is getting in the way of their willingness to make changes and seeking support to work through this. Taking a systemic approach requires that *everyone* understands the relevance of their actions and decisions to the change process.

Successful organisations simultaneously promote both stability and change (Burchell & Kolb, 2006), consistent with the notion of adaptive expertise introduced in Chapter Two (Bransford, Derry, Berliner, & Hammerness, 2005). There is need for an increased focus on prioritising what change matters and how much is too much. When prioritising change, close attention should be paid to creating and maintaining coherence across professional learning opportunities. This should be accompanied by high expectations of change within an environment of trust that supports necessary risk taking. Finally, talk is needed in terms of evaluating the processes and outcomes of change. By engaging in less change, but building the capability to evaluate the extent to which prioritised change has actually occurred, professional learning might become a more effective lever for improving valued outcomes for students.

> The ultimate measure of the effectiveness of change needs to be improved valued outcomes for students.

Reflection questions

QUESTION 1

Using the descriptions in the framework for the four dimensions in Figure 4.1, decide whether your school is basic, mixed/middle or integrated.
Record and discuss the evidence on which you based your judgements.

a. Identifying priorities (Table 4.1)

BASIC	MIDDLE/MIXED	INTEGRATED

b. Holding high expectations (Table 4.2)

BASIC	MIDDLE/MIXED	INTEGRATED

c. Communicating challenges (Tables 4.3, 4.4 and 4.5)

BASIC	MIDDLE/MIXED	INTEGRATED

d. Evaluating outcomes (Table 4.6)

BASIC	MIDDLE/MIXED	INTEGRATED

QUESTION 2

What aspects of change knowledge is your school most competent in? Why do you think this is the case?

QUESTION 3

How might you use the framework to help leaders and teachers in your school to develop capacity in talking about change and, ultimately, in implementing effective change?

References

Bransford, J., Derry, S., Berliner, D., & Hammerness, I. (2005). Theories of learning and their roles in teaching. In L. Darling-Hammond & J. Bransford (Eds.), *Preparing teachers for a changing world* (pp. 40–87). San Francisco: John Wiley & Sons.

Bryk, A. S., & Schneider, B. (2002). *Trust in schools: A core resource for improvement*. New York: Russell Sage Foundation.

Bryk, A. S., Sebring, P. B., Kerbow, D., Rollow, S., & Easton, J. Q. (1998). *Charting Chicago school reform: Democratic localism as a lever for change*. Boulder, CO: Westview Press.

Burchell, N., & Kolb, D. (2006). Stability and change for stability. *University of Auckland Business Review, Spring*, 33–41.

Elmore, R. (2004). *School reform from the inside out: Policy, practice and performance*. Cambridge, MA: Harvard Education Press.

Good, T. L. (1987). Two decades of research on teacher expectations: Findings and new directions. *Journal of Teacher Education, 38*(4), 32–47.

O'Connell, P. (2009). *Is sustainability of schooling improvement an article of faith or can it be deliberately crafted?* Unpublished doctoral thesis, The University of Auckland, Auckland.

Robinson, V. M. J., Lloyd, C., & Rowe, K. (2008). The impact of leadership on student outcomes. An analysis of the differential effects of leadership types. *Educational Administration Quarterly, 44*(5), 635–674.

Schon, D. (1983). *The reflective practitioner: How professionals think in action*. New York: Basic Books.

CHAPTER FIVE

Whakapakari Kura: Learning and Inquiry in Māori-Medium Education

Margie Hōhepa

This chapter focuses on some of the challenges for Māori-medium education in the process of building better schools. It considers important questions relating to how inquiry could best be conducted in these settings, the nature of relevant evidence and, therefore, the appropriate standards for Māori-medium education. Why is such a discussion important? In Chapter Two, "Towards an Optimal Model for Building Better Schools", it was argued that in any schooling improvement approach there are features that are particularly significant to the context. Māori-medium education is one such feature, which makes it important to consider explicitly Māori-medium settings in any discussion of how evidence, inquiry and standards might be woven together to improve schooling in our national education system.

This chapter argues that such a weaving task requires particular sorts of knowledge and understanding, encompassing the kaupapa (philosophies) and aspirations that underpin Māori-medium settings as well as the student outcomes that are valued. The kaupapa and aspirations underpinning Māori-medium education include both Māori language and cultural regeneration, along with what might be considered more general educational outcomes (Smith, 1997). It is not an either/or choice between language and cultural achievement and educational achievement, but rather the development of both.

In terms of the process of inquiry, and the development of related professional learning capabilities for teachers and leaders, there are features of the Māori-medium context that are significant. For example, theoretical knowledge about effective approaches for bilingual teaching and learning are required. This knowledge needs to be understood in light of the fact that Māori-medium provision is a relatively recent development, aimed at producing graduates who are bilingually and biculturally competent. Similarly, it needs to be understood that the Māori-medium curriculum, and associated pedagogical and assessment-related tools, are at varying levels of development. This knowledge and understanding help to identify the range of evidence that may be needed when making decisions about what practices work and what needs to change. In terms of change, we need to consider not only how to bring about change but also why it is needed.

To ensure that robust processes of inquiry using a range of evidence take place, and the necessary changes do occur, effective leadership for Māori-medium education is key. Chapter One highlighted the fact that educational leaders who promote and participate in teacher learning have the greatest impact on student outcomes (Robinson, Hōhepa, & Lloyd, 2009). How leaders approach this task with regard to Māori-medium education is critical to improving Māori-medium student outcomes. In predominantly English-medium schools offering Māori-medium instruction, the school leadership may not explicitly include representation from the Māori-medium setting. In these situations, school leadership participation in and promotion of Māori-medium teacher learning often ends up being relatively invisible as well. Three points need to be taken on board:
- the importance of school leadership being inclusive of Māori-medium education leadership
- the importance of school leaders participating alongside and promoting the professional learning of Māori-medium teachers
- the importance of leadership that knows what is going on in relation to its Māori-medium teachers.

The last two points are relevant not only for settings with both Māori- and English-medium provision but also for Māori-medium-only school settings.

In Māori-medium settings the school community, or kura whānau, generally includes parents, staff, students and the wider community. Schooling improvement work necessarily includes support for the aspirations and goals of school communities for their students. The building of better Māori-medium schooling involves taking into account the extent to which kura whānau goals for student achievement include valued linguistic and cultural outcomes. A major challenge is to raise student achievement in Māori-medium education in ways that enhance Māori language and cultural development and avoid substituting one for the other.

A major challenge to building better schools involves raising student achievement in Māori-medium education in ways that enhance Māori language and cultural development.

Such aspirations might best be understood in terms of the overarching strategic outcome in *Ka Hikitia*, the Māori education strategy for 2008–2012: "Māori enjoying education success as Māori" (Ministry of Education, 2008). This outcome links directly to the main emphasis of *Te Marautanga o Aotearoa* (Ministry of Education, 2007a), which is the partner document to *The New Zealand Curriculum* (Ministry of Education, 2007b) for Māori-medium settings at immersion levels 1 and 2 (described below). While containing many parallels, *Te Marautanga* is not a direct translation of *The New Zealand Curriculum* and has been developed in cognisance of Māori philosophies and principles.[2] *Te Marautanga* aims to ensure that students in Māori-medium settings develop skills and knowledge that will enable them to participate in and contribute to te iwi Māori (Māori society) and the wider world. Like *The New Zealand Curriculum*, *Te Marautanga* draws on "an inquiry learning and knowledge creation cycle"—"Te hurihanga whakaako pakirehua me te waihanga mātauranga"—(p. 16), as a process to help Māori-medium schools and classrooms to develop a school-based curriculum with kura whānau, so that it reflects both the essential learning outcomes for students from *Te Marautanga* and from the community.

Chapter One noted that standards have already been introduced to English-medium schools in Aotearoa New Zealand, and also alluded to some of the debates and questions that have arisen. At the time of writing this book, Māori-medium standards—whanaketanga rumaki Māori (literally, development immersion Māori)—are being trialled in some Māori-medium schools in 2010. The introduction of standards into the Māori medium not only raises similar debates and questions as

2 http://nzcurriculum.tki.org.nz/Curriculum-documents/Te-Marautanga-o-Aotearoa

those identified in Chapter One, but also some that are more specific to indigenous-language schooling programmes. The picture is made more complex by the fact that Māori-medium education is not one context, but multiple contexts. These multiple contexts are represented in the range of provisions identified below:

- level 1: (81 percent to 100 percent immersion)—maintenance programmes in which Māori is the principal language of communication and instruction, and the principal curriculum[3] is taught entirely in Māori
- level 2: (51 percent to 80 percent immersion)—development programmes in which Māori is the language of communication and instruction for most of the time
- level 3: (31 percent to 50 percent immersion)—emerging programmes in which English is the main language of communication and instruction
- level 4: (12 percent to 30 percent immersion)—essentially English-medium programmes that incorporate between three and 7.5 hours of teaching in Māori.

The next section discusses where Māori medium might fit in the process of inquiry and improvement. The key messages for the effective inclusion of Māori-medium education draw on the work of the Building Evaluative Capability in Schooling Improvement Project.

"Māori-medium education" is a term used to identify a range of provisions that use Māori as a language of instruction for an identified percentage of the time. Many of the provisions operate within explicit cultural and philosophical guidelines.

Defining Māori-medium education

Te reo Māori (the Māori language) is the language of the indigenous people of Aotearoa New Zealand. Māori-medium education involves delivering curriculum subjects other than te reo Māori in both Māori and English, or in Māori only. Māori-medium settings may comprise either an entire school, or a number of classrooms within a school that also has classrooms delivering the curriculum through the medium of English. Thus the term "Māori-medium education" spans a range of schooling provisions in which Māori language is a medium of instruction.

---

3 www.minedu.govt.nz/.../Schedule_1_Definitition_of_Levels_of_Maori_Immersion.aspx. The definition of levels of Māori immersion refer to the principal curriculum. We take this to mean the national curriculum and/or marautanga. "Emerging programmes" also refers to those in which "an increase in the level of immersion is restricted by the level of fluency of the teacher".

The provisions include kura kaupapa Māori (schools underpinned by Māori philosophy), wharekura (kaupapa Māori secondary schooling), kura iwi (literally, tribal schools), rumaki (immersion schools or classrooms) and reorua (bilingual schools or classrooms). Many kura kaupapa Māori and wharekura operate within explicit cultural and philosophical guidelines, such as those laid down in *Te Aho Matua*, the kura kaupapa Māori movement's founding document (Education (Te Aho Matua) Amendment Act, 1999). Kura iwi may operate within specific iwi frameworks as well as through te reo Māori (Ministry of Education, 2008).

Learners in bilingual classes or schools are involved in Māori-medium education for three to 20 hours per week. Learners in immersion classes or schools are involved in Māori-medium education for 20¼ to 25 hours a week (Ministry of Education, 2009). In 2007, 408 schools provided some form of Māori-medium education to nearly 26,000 students; 11,000 in immersion classes or schools and over 18,000 in bilingual classes or schools. Over 6,000 of these students were in kura kaupapa Māori.

Building better Māori-medium schooling in mixed settings

Schools that include both English-medium and Māori-medium educational settings can find it challenging to ensure that Māori-medium settings are included effectively in schooling improvement work. There is a need to consider what outcomes are valued in each setting, the kinds of leadership positioning that are appropriate and the nature of professional learning. When Māori-medium education is part of a school, the school's goals for improvement need to be such that they align with Māori-medium kaupapa and with cultural and linguistic goals valued in their Māori-medium classrooms. Ideally, in such schools explicit consideration of Māori-medium education should occur as a normal part of its inquiry processes into the effectiveness of current practices. This calls for the school as a whole to have knowledge about and understanding of the specific kaupapa or philosophy underpinning its Māori-medium education programme. It also calls for a shared understanding about what is realistically achievable with regard to the level of immersion at which the curriculum is delivered. This will help to locate goals for Māori-medium education student achievement in terms of both Māori-medium educational aspirations and current realities.

Schools with Māori-medium education need to ensure they have shared knowledge about the underpinning kaupapa, aspirations and student outcomes valued by the whānau.

Alignment should also reflect theoretical understanding of the effective approaches for bilingual teaching and learning (May, Hill, & Tiakiwai, 2006). This understanding is important so that a school's work plans and professional development plans for raising student achievement in its Māori-medium education classrooms are informed by evidence of what is likely to work in bilingual or immersion settings.

When a school includes both Māori-medium-education and English-medium-education settings, this should be reflected in its leadership; that is, the school leadership team should specifically include Māori-medium-education leadership. This will help to ensure that Māori-medium educational matters are on the school's "formal agenda", so to speak. It also helps to ensure that leadership of the school's inquiry processes includes important knowledge and understanding of Māori-medium education. If these things don't happen, there may be a number of cost implications further along the track for the school, in terms of time, relationships and developing and funding additional or alternative professional development for Māori-medium staff.

> Māori-medium education needs to be included in school leadership and on the formal agenda.

The potential opportunities for and costs of different professional development arrangements involving Māori-medium staff require careful identification and examination through schooling improvement work. Varying arrangements present different opportunities and costs, in terms of interdependence, capability, time and relationships. There are opportunities for developing interdependence when Māori- and English-medium staff work together. These opportunities may, for instance, increase Māori-medium capability by improving generic knowledge about teaching pedagogy and assessment, as Māori-medium teachers work alongside English-medium colleagues with English-medium education expertise. This expertise may be internal or external. English-medium capability to develop more effective Māori programmes and better support for Māori students may also be increased as a result of working with Māori-medium colleagues.

The costs may involve the time and energy required for Māori-medium staff to transfer English-medium-focused learning so that it is relevant to, among other things, Māori as the language of instruction, Māori-medium-education goals, bilingual learning patterns and the needs of the students. This process involves more than a simple translation. Professional development arrangements for Māori-medium staff may need to factor in formally the time and opportunities for this transfer to take place, rather than expecting or assuming staff will be able to manage this on top of their day-to-day work (Earl, Timperley, & Stewart, 2008).

There are also opportunities and costs involved where Māori-medium staff within a school are working independently of their counterparts in English medium. Opportunities include being able to take a single focus on the teaching and learning needs in Māori-medium classrooms. There is also the opportunity to recognise explicitly rangatiratanga dimensions that so often underpin Māori-medium developments. Rangatiratanga can include values such as Māori self-determination or the notion of "by Māori for Māori". However, there is a danger of benign neglect by leadership teams masquerading as recognition of rangatiratanga, resulting in costs that include isolation, and limited possibilities for effective inquiry cycles and for the development of effective learning communities—particularly if there are only one or two Māori-medium staff.

Separate opportunities for professional learning can also have implications for the development of relational trust. The importance of trust in building better schooling is discussed in Chapter Two. It is more challenging to build such trust across cultures and languages than when the basics of these are shared and when separate professional learning opportunities are provided. The extent to which relational trust is developed has been shown to have a strong relationship to the degree of success of schooling improvement efforts (Bryk & Schneider, 2002).

Developing trust has been observed to be more difficult in diverse communities. The reason for this may be simply that it is easier to trust those who are more similar to oneself (Tschannen-Moran & Hoy, 2000). This issue applies just as much to relationships within schools as across schools, where different provisions are driven by different educational and cultural imperatives. What this may mean is that developing relational trust can be a particularly complex task when a school spans a range of educational provisions with differing priorities. Leaders in culturally and educationally heterogeneous contexts may need to take the initiative in building relational trust (Robinson et al., 2009). The development of strong relational trust, coupled with improved outcomes in areas of achievement that are important to Māori-medium and English-medium settings, can lead to members coming to know they can work together well. Relational trust can then be drawn on as a resource when looking at further areas for development that include both Māori and English medium.

> In contexts that span a range of educational provisions with differing priorities, developing relational trust may be a particularly complex task that requires active leadership.

Building relational trust involves working out how to work together in ways that make a difference across all settings in a school, and that preserve the integrity of all those settings. These ways of working involve developing and maintaining relationships through flexible arrangements that enable access to and sharing of knowledge for mutual benefit. Some approaches to schooling improvement have resulted in teachers in Māori-medium education participating in ways that do not engender or reflect developing relational trust, including:

- teachers in Māori-medium settings participate, but their needs are largely ignored and their participation in improvement activities is relatively invisible
- teachers in Māori-medium settings informally opt out of professional development activities because they are not seen as relevant
- Māori-medium teachers participate in activities related to an English-medium focus and also participate in professional development for Māori medium that does not relate to the school development focus
- Māori-medium teachers participate in professional development that does acknowledge Māori-medium needs, but then they are relatively invisible in meetings, learning discussions, data analysis, etc.
- Māori-medium teachers conclude that their needs will not be met through current activities, and they either (a) negotiate parallel or separate Māori-medium-education targeted activities (which may or may not provide Māori-medium assessment data to the school-wide data); (b) formally opt out; or (c) formally opt out and negotiate an alternative professional development focus.

Māori-medium-only settings

The major premise of this book is that inquiry using a range of evidence is key to building the kinds of schools that promote all student learning. This approach involves focusing on the strengths and learning needs of students, teachers and leaders. Māori-medium approaches to education focus on strengthening student achievement and enhancing development in te reo Māori, mātauranga Māori (Māori knowledge) and whānau. Māori-medium-education provision is relatively new, and various programmes can be at any number of points of development, including the initial establishment phase; in the case of kura kaupapa Māori, this may involve a kura being in a teina (satellite) relationship with a tuakana (established kura) while awaiting official recognition, or in the process of physically building permanent accommodation.

Recognition of the diversity within and across the different provisions that fall under the umbrella term "Māori medium" is critical in order to support the building of better Māori-medium schooling. Just as one size does not fit across Māori- and English-medium provisions, a one-size approach is not appropriate for Māori medium (or English medium for that matter). Just as English-medium professional development does not necessarily apply to the Māori medium, we cannot expect to take a Māori-medium generic approach and expect it to be appropriate, without considering the specific aspirations and goals underpinning a particular setting.

Māori-medium whānau or school communities view their school leadership as a key driver for realising their specific aspirations. School leadership in these contexts often goes wider than the principal and teaching staff, encompassing other key whānau members as well. This can involve other whānau members being actively involved in decisions that relate to student learning and, more generally, in the running of the school (Robinson et al., 2009).

Given the kinds of aspirations for student learning that Māori-medium kura tend to embrace, Māori-medium leaders' duties and accountabilities tend to encompass a broad definition of achievement, which may not stop with students and can often extend to the kura whānau (particularly parents) and into wider Māori society. Leadership in Māori-medium education encompasses a range of roles, including being:

• a representative and advocate for Māori-medium provision
• a supporter and educational leader—not only for staff and students within the school gate but also for the wider whānau
• a leader of wider cultural, educational or political movements.

If these roles primarily rest with one person, or a small group, then overload and burn-out are real and ever-present dangers. An accompanying danger is that tasks entailed in the educational leadership role get swamped by other duties. The question of how to ensure that Māori-medium educational leadership stays focused on core business is not an easy one, as the examples above are arguably all central to Māori-medium educational agendas. If, however, the immediate goal involves strengthening teaching and learning in particular ways in order to raise student achievement, then it is imperative that strategies be found that enable leaders to lead this. Enacting much-valued Māori metaphors might be one effective strategy; for example, "Nāu te pāro, nāku te pāro, ka ora te iwi"—with your food basket and my food basket the people will flourish—can call into play shared leadership, leaving specific educational leadership tasks related to a prioritised achievement area for the most skilled. These leadership tasks may also include identifying and gathering relevant evidence, overseeing inquiry processes, observing and critiquing teaching and so on in the "food baskets" of the tumuaki (principal) and senior management, with other able whānau members picking up core tasks related to other no-less-important learning areas.

Māori-medium teachers are likely to reflect more rather than less diversity when compared with English-medium teachers. There is more likely to be a range of teacher education qualifications at different levels, which may or may not include specific preparation for Māori medium. There are also likely to be differences in prior teaching experience, again which may or may not include Māori medium. Levels of diversity across Māori-medium staff require recognition when identifying teacher learning needs and identifying actions that might be required to address these needs (Earl et al., 2008).

What counts as evidence in Māori-medium education?

As well as the knowledge bases and languages focused on during professional development, the knowledge bases and languages in which students are assessed also need explicit consideration when identifying evidence about learning and for use in inquiry. Information gathered from formal schooling improvement projects indicates that it is not unusual for the focus of improvement work to be on achievement in English across a school's Māori-medium and English-medium provisions (Hōhepa, 2009). In this work, English-language assessment tools relating to the focus were found to be used in some Māori-medium classrooms. It is not unreasonable to expect that schooling improvement work in classrooms operating at immersion levels 1 and 2 in which Māori is the language of instruction for at least half the time would focus on raising student achievement in and through te reo Māori. However, indications are that activities in level 2 immersion Māori-medium education settings are as likely to involve raising students' achievement in English, reflected through an emphasis on assessing learning using English-language assessment tools.

Given the above, there is a danger that a major role for level 2 immersion (often described as "bilingual") may become one of supporting English-medium achievement at the expense of supporting student achievement in the context of Māori language and cultural regeneration. There is evidence that this may also be the case in some level 1 immersion classrooms. If schools with Māori-medium classrooms set goals and organise professional learning opportunities that focus on achievement in English only, they will also need to consider the impact this might have on teachers and students in these Māori-medium settings and whether this focus might undermine kaupapa and goals. For example, if teaching practice is to be improved only in relation to English-medium delivery and achievement, how does this affect the proportion of time Māori is used for instruction, and students' Māori achievement in Māori-medium settings? If student achievement is monitored in English only, how does this monitoring affect students' learning in te reo Māori? Decisions about such things as teacher instruction and monitoring achievement need to take cognisance of the level of immersion and the type of provision in Māori-medium educational settings.

A focus on English in Māori-medium education, especially if students are faced with transitions to English-medium education, is not problematic in itself (Rau, 2005). Indeed, goals relating to the development of bilingual competencies are explicitly stated in *Te Aho Matua*. When deliberately planned for and delivered appropriately, a focus on English literacy— be it as a means to realise bilingual aspirations expressed in *Te Aho Matua*, or in preparation for transition to English-medium education, or both—can support and even enhance the development of Māori language and literacy (Berryman & Glynn, 2003). However, where there is an almost singular focus on English literacy assessments, it has been difficult to identify from available data the impact of schooling improvement activities on students' learning in te reo Māori (Hōhepa, 2009).

> When deliberately planned for and delivered appropriately, a focus on achievement in English can support and even enhance the development of Māori-language achievement.

The reason for this situation is that theories of action position Māori-medium education (and other forms of bilingual education) as being primarily about improving student achievement in the English language. The resulting plans and activities may undermine important language and cultural goals underpinning Māori-medium education. A similar result may occur when Māori-medium education is seen as essentially the same as English-medium education except for the language of instruction. In these situations, little deliberate consideration is given to how Māori-medium-education student achievement in Māori might also be effectively raised.

A clear measure of Māori-medium education visibility (or invisibility) is the degree to which evidence of Māori-medium students' achievement in te reo Māori is collected, analysed and reported. None of the schools in clusters (which included Māori- and English-medium settings) for which assessment data were provided for the Building Evaluative Capability in Schooling Improvement Project (Hōhepa, 2009) included data from Māori-language assessments (e.g., AKA, the Māori-language version of the School Entry Assessment, asTTle Māori), despite the available information indicating that there were a number of schools that offered Māori-medium programmes at immersion levels 1 and 2.

A possible explanation for the lack of Māori-medium assessment data may be that assessment can become a high-stakes activity for indigenous language programmes such as Māori-medium education (Rau, 2008). Developments relating to standards will need to take cognisance of this issue. The introduction of standards in Aotearoa New Zealand needs to be mindful of the negative effects that high-stakes approaches, such as that taken in the United States educational policy No Child Left Behind, have had on indigenous schooling programmes and initiatives. The pressure to devote instructional time to areas that are tested in English only has been at the expense of other areas, including indigenous language and cultural instruction (Beaulieu, Sparks, & Alonzo, 2005; McCarty, 2009; Romero-Little, 2006). There is also evidence of little gap reduction for indigenous groups, coupled with evidence of declining scores on standardised tests (McCarty, 2009).

> Assessment can become a high-stakes activity for indigenous language programmes such as those defined as Māori-medium. education.

Concerns and challenges relating to the potential high-stakes nature of Māori-medium-education data sit in tension with processes of professional inquiry (shown in Figure 1.1) that are aimed at raising student achievement, and looking for evidence of this through the use of fit-for-purpose assessment tools. Identifying and addressing teaching and learning needs, and working with assessment findings in order to do this, requires not only careful management of challenge and trust, as discussed in Chapters One and Four, but also consideration of safety, particularly in terms of the uses to which the data are put. If Māori-medium-education settings are to learn through the collection and use of evidence in the form of achievement data, the data themselves require safe management so that Māori-medium education as a movement does not get "burnt"—be it a perception or an actuality—by inappropriate data use and reporting.

Safety also includes ensuring that assessment evidence is not misused as a weapon against Māori-medium education as a provision, at the school or national level. Challenges like these may be addressed in at least two ways. One is by ensuring assessments are administered and analysed properly during the various phases of inquiry. Another is by deliberately planning for the development of assessment-related knowledge and skills (and possibly assessment tools themselves) as part of the inquiry process. If teachers are developing knowledge about assessments, or if the assessment tools are being further developed and refined, then any interpretation, reporting or other uses of the data need to take such developmental aspects into account explicitly (which may be what is happening currently, and may help to explain the lack of Māori-medium-education data in the Building Evaluative Capability in Schooling Improvement Project).

The approach being taken to standards in Aotearoa New Zealand attempts to address the above issues by including both English and te reo Māori. There has been acknowledgement that there is a smaller existing evidence base, fewer assessment tools and potentially less familiarity among teachers in using evidence and such tools for Māori-medium education when compared with what is already in place to support the development and use of English-medium standards. Work on ngā whanaketanga rumaki Māori, the standards for Māori medium, has been located within a wider work programme to strengthen Māori-medium education, including support for rolling out *Te Marautanga* and addressing gaps in literacy and numeracy assessment tools for Māori-medium settings.

A challenge that needs to be addressed explicitly in the new standards environment relates to what counts as valued student outcomes for Māori medium, and the extent to which ngā whanaketanga rumaki Māori support and protect these. In Chapter One it was noted that English-medium standards focus on reading, writing and mathematics, and that these are fundamental to accessing the curriculum. Māori-medium standards focus on the equivalent areas—pāngarau (numeracy), tuhituhi (writing) and pānui (reading)—and an additional area, kōrero (oral language). Particularly given the inclusion of kōrero, there is potential for Māori-medium standards to be used to identify students' learning needs in ways that reinforce the critical importance of language and cultural learning. There is also less potential for standards to result in a narrow refocusing of instruction if the emphasis is put on pānui, tuhituhi and pāngarau at the expense of other areas of the curriculum. The second scenario is less likely to occur if the kaupapa (philosophies) and aspirations that underpin Māori-medium settings are kept to the foreground. Some thought will undoubtedly need to be given to how best to gather evidence on cultural and/or iwi-related learning at school and national levels.

Implications for learning in Māori-medium education

The extent to which Māori-medium education, and the accompanying learning needs, is considered similar to or different from English-medium education has implications for how Māori-medium settings are positioned in efforts to build better schools. If the needs of Māori-medium education are considered similar to those of English-medium education, then the approach taken may be one size fits all. A typical scenario is that the only professional learning opportunities for Māori-medium educators are those available to their English-medium colleagues. An assumption linked with this approach appears to be that it is easy for Māori-medium teachers to transfer what is learnt in relation to English-medium to Māori-medium education. In this scenario, little cognisance is given to issues relating to bilingual or second-language development, to learning pathways and progressions for these, or to cultural factors (Rau, 2005, 2008). Both these scenarios are likely to be detrimental to achieving the aspirations of Māori-medium education.

If Māori-medium education is seen as being a significant schooling provision, which comes in diverse forms and with a range of different needs, then it follows that there need to be opportunities to:

- discuss schooling improvement in relation to different Māori-medium provisions (e.g., Is there a different focus for different levels of immersion? Does the focus for higher immersion settings that teach predominantly through Māori language need to be on Māori language achievement? Why, or why not?)
- examine the extent to which the delivery of professional development takes Māori-medium settings into account (e.g., Is a generic approach or a targeted approach focused on the language of instruction preferable, and why? How can culture and language as defining features of Māori-medium settings best be addressed when providing professional development?)
- in mixed school settings where Māori-medium settings have a parallel work plan to English-medium settings or are working independently (e.g., where they have regrouped around a separate programme as a Māori-medium group), consider what each needs to know about the other (e.g., Why should English

and Māori medium know and understand each other's goals, activities and achievement outcomes?)

• consider what Māori-medium evidence should look like (e.g., How does it acknowledge and reflect language and cultural goals? What kinds of data on Māori-language achievement should be collected or considered, and why? How should Māori-language assessment data be used in monitoring and reporting activities, and by whom? What issues need to be addressed, such as those related to challenge or safety around Māori-language assessment data?).

Four of the themes discussed in this chapter—identifying outcomes, leadership structures, professional development and school development—have been formulated into a continuum describing points at the basic, middle/mixed and integrated levels (see Table 5.1). These descriptions are designed to provide points of reflection for those in both Māori and English medium where they see benefits in working together. This situation may arise within a school that offers both media of instruction, or across schools when working together in some kind of clustering arrangement.

Table 5.1 A continuum of capabilities when Māori- and English-medium education settings work together within schools or across schools

Dimension	Basic	Middle/mixed	Integrated
Identifying valued outcomes	There is some awareness that outcomes valued for Māori-medium education (MME) might be different from those for English-medium education (EME), but actions indicate they are to be similar, with little discussion of the implications.	There is some acknowledgement of differences in the outcomes valued, but only superficial attempts are made to understand the cultural and linguistic goals valued for MME, or to ensure they form part of ongoing actions.	A systematic inquiry is undertaken to identify outcomes valued for students in both settings, with knowledge of the cultural and linguistic goals valued in MME forming the basis of inquiry.

Leadership	The focus for MME leaders is seen to be in MME settings.	MME leaders are included at the level seen to be appropriate to the size of the MME unit (e.g., senior teachers).	MME leaders are part of the school leadership team to ensure MME matters are on the formal agenda in ways that are acceptable to the MME whānau/ community.
Professional development	MME staff attend EME professional development and collegial discussions, with the expectation that information can be translated into MME settings. There is no discussion of costs or benefits.	MME staff choose whether they attend EME professional development or MME-specific professional development, with little discussion of the associated costs and benefits.	There is full discussion of when it is appropriate for EME and MME to engage in joint professional development efforts and work together, and when it is appropriate to work separately with knowledge of aspirations of MME and cognisance taken of the need to learn from one another.
School development	It is assumed that one size fits all, with no discussion of how different approaches might fit different language and cultural schooling provisions.	Different focuses and approaches are discussed, but without a deep understanding of the cultural and linguistic aspirations of MME. MME may engage in different work from EME.	Both similar and different focuses and approaches are discussed from the perspective of deep understanding of different cultural and language aspirations and consideration of what each needs to know about and from the other.

Reflection questions

If your kura/school has, or is considering having, classrooms that use Māori as the medium of instruction, the following questions are some you may like to discuss or reflect on.

QUESTION 1

Which documents (e.g., *Te Marautanga o Aotearoa*, *The New Zealand Curriculum for English Medium Teaching and Learning*, *Te Reo Māori in the New Zealand Curriculum*) are used to guide the delivery of the curriculum in Māori-medium classrooms, and why?

QUESTION 2

What kinds of evidence does your kura/school collect to demonstrate achievement for students in classrooms that use Māori as the medium of instruction?

QUESTION 3

How are the whanaketanga rumaki Māori and/or the mathematics, reading and writing standards going to be used with Māori-medium students?

QUESTION 4

What kinds of discussions do your kura whānau (school community, including staff, parents, students) have about the implications of English instruction on the development and maintenance of student competence in te reo Māori?

References

Beaulieu, D., Sparks, L., & Alonzo, M. (2005). *Preliminary report on No Child Left Behind in Indian country.* Washington, DC: National Indian Education Association.

Berryman, M., & Glynn, T. (2003). *Transition from Māori to English: A community approach.* Wellington: New Zealand Council for Educational Research.

Bryk, A. S., & Schneider, B. L. (2002). *Trust in schools: A core resource for improvement.* New York: Sage Foundation Publications.

Earl, L., Timperley, H., & Stewart, G. (2008, October). *Learning from the QTR&D programme: Findings of the external evaluation.* Aphoria Consulting Ltd. Retrieved from http://www.educationcounts.govt.nz/publications/curriculum/49172

Education (Te Aho Matua) Amendment Act 1999. Available at: http://www.legislation.govt.nz/act/public/1999/0079/latest/DLM31205.html

Hōhepa, M. (2009). Māori medium education. In *Milestone 5: Contract research report to the Ministry of Education, June 2005* (pp. 153–163). Auckland: Auckland UniServices.

May, S., Hill, R., & Tiakiwai, S. (2006). *Bilingual education in Aotearoa/New Zealand: Key findings from bilingual/immersion education: Indicators of good practice.* Wellington: Ministry of Education.

McCarty, T. (2009). The impact of high-stakes accountability policies on Native American learners: Evidence from research. *Teaching Education, 20*(1), 7–29.

Ministry of Education. (2007a). *Te marautanga o Aotearoa: He tauira hei kōrerorero.* Wellington: Learning Media.

Ministry of Education. (2007b). *The New Zealand curriculum.* Wellington: Learning Media.

Ministry of Education. (2008*). Ka hikitia—managing for success: The Māori Education Strategy 2008–2012.* Wellington: Author.

Ministry of Education. (2009). *Ngā haeata mātauranga 2007/08.* Wellington: Author.

Rau, C. (2005). Literacy acquisition, assessment and achievement of year two students in total immersion in Māori programmes. *International Journal of Bilingual Education and Bilingualism, 8*(5), 404–432.

Rau, C. (2008). Assessment in indigenous language programmes. In E. Shohamy & H. Hornberger (Eds.), *Encyclopedia of language and education: Volume 7: Language testing and assessment* (2nd ed., pp. 319–330). New York: Springer Science+Business Media LLC.

Robinson, V., Hōhepa, M., & Lloyd, C. (2009). *School leadership and student outcomes: Identifying what works and why: Best evidence synthesis iteration*. Wellington: Ministry of Education.

Romero-Little, M. (2006). Honoring our own: Rethinking indigenous languages and literacy. *Anthropology and Educational Quarterly, 37*(4), 399–402.

Smith, G. H. (1997). *The development of kaupapa Māori: Theory and praxis.* Unpublished PhD thesis, The University of Auckland, Auckland.

Tschannen-Moran, M., & Hoy, W. K. (2000). A multidisciplinary analysis of the nature, meaning, and measurement of trust. *Review of Educational Research, 70*(4), 547–593.

PART
THREE

INQUIRY USING EVIDENCE

CHAPTER SIX

Inquiry Into Classroom Practice for Improvement

Judy Parr

Inquiry into classroom practice has two broad, interrelated purposes. The first involves teacher inquiry into student learning. The idea here is to work out where a student currently is in relation to the performance desired, and then what has to happen to move learning forward. An integral part of the purpose of this kind of inquiry in the classroom should be to help teachers to scaffold and support students' inquiry into their own learning. The other broad thrust of classroom inquiry involves evaluating the extent to which current practice (and then "new" practice) is effective in meeting the learning needs of students. Stemming from the findings of this inquiry is further consideration by teachers into what *they* might need to learn in relation to the practices known to be effective to meet the learning needs of their students.

Research on building better schools suggests that school-level inquiry—which should include the classroom level—is often not a very robust part of the inquiry cycle (as outlined in Chapter One). There are links that need strengthening. These links concern the extent and nature of the relationship between the evidence of student learning and classroom practice.

The first evidence-to-practice link is that between the information obtained from an assessment of learning and the instructional decision that follows. It relates to knowing what the pattern of information from the diagnostic assessment means in terms of putting in place appropriate practice to enhance achievement. The other link from evidence to practice that needs to be strengthened involves the systematic investigation into the relationship between particular practices in the classroom (and associated teacher knowledge) and the pattern of student achievement outcomes. To explain patterns in achievement within a school or year level, or a group of students, data on practice need to be collected in a similar way across classrooms.

With respect to the first point, it is a highly skilled task to relate the pattern of achievement to specific instruction. Such actions are the litmus test of the adaptive expert. In our research on schooling improvement we asked teachers to spell out the chain of events from what was learnt about a student or group of students from an assessment, to the specific teaching or instructional moves that would follow. More specifically, we asked them to think about a recent assessment and to record specific things they had found out about the learning and achievement of a student. Then we asked what instructional decisions they had made, and, finally, how they would know if the moves they had decided on were effective. In a number of cases the instructional practices teachers said they decided on failed to align with the description of the characteristics of the student's learning they had recorded. It would seem that this link from evidence to practice is a particularly challenging one to make.

With respect to the second point—obtaining systematic data about practice across classrooms—our research suggests that although observations of classroom practice are often undertaken by leaders, the information obtained is not always comparable across teachers in the same school. Often, too, the information obtained is not necessarily specifically related to the focus of improvement efforts that have been put in place in response to student achievement data, so it cannot be used to make inferences about the success of professional development or particular practices. Both of these links involving evidence to practice are discussed in the following sections.

In inquiry in the classroom, evidence-to-practice links need strengthening.

If inquiry and building evaluative capability at the classroom level were operating optimally, we would expect to see the knowledge and actions that are discussed in this chapter operating at a high level. What key actions might look like at different levels of evaluative expertise is described in the chapter through a series of progressions, sometimes amplified with a short case vignette. The knowledge and actions are considered from the perspective of the inquiry cycle.

Identifying valued outcomes, where students are in relation to them and student learning needs

Basically, identifying valued outcomes and student learning needs involves three actions:

- agreeing, as a school community, on what the valued outcomes for student learning are
- ascertaining where the students in each teacher's classroom are placed in relation to the goals associated with the outcomes
- identifying what students need to know and do to achieve these outcomes (the nature of the gap between current learning and desired learning).

These outcomes generally—but not exclusively (see, for example, the discussion in Chapter Five on Māori-medium education)—relate to the curriculum and/or normative expectations. An example of national expectations is encapsulated in the achievement standards in literacy and numeracy. It is important to reiterate periodically what these goals are to avoid the trap of the assessment instruments or standards alone defining the goals by default. One schooling improvement cluster we worked with realised in a discussion session that their valued outcomes for reading were not simply encapsulated in an average performance of stanine 4 on STAR. They wanted their students to read widely for pleasure, to be engaged, to see the purpose of reading and to be skilled in strategy use. They needed additional ways of finding out how their students were going in relation to these outcomes they valued. They realised that to some extent they had let the assessment instrument determine their goals or valued outcomes. The revisiting of valued outcomes in reading was important to prevent a narrowing of the curriculum—in this case, a narrowing of the definition of reading.

Finding out where students are in order to move learning forward requires specific information of a particular nature. Knowing that a student is at a certain curriculum level or two years behind their age cohort is important, but not helpful diagnostically. It does not provide sufficient information about a student's strengths and gaps to know what to build on. A detailed profile of student achievement is required to assist with the diagnosis of learning needs. The profile is also important to identify strengths, because these may provide building blocks for new learning.

Information about performance at more than one point in time should be obtained so that not only the current state but also the previous condition can be seen. Only then can the trajectory of learning, in terms of rate of progress, be evaluated. An important part of the decision relating to need concerns pace of learning: how quickly do students need to acquire this learning? This is an essential consideration for students who have not made progress at the expected rate. If they don't start to make accelerated progress, they are going to fall further behind their peers. To keep an eye on this, some class teachers and syndicates employ visual techniques. They locate each individual student on a point on a graph at the different assessment times. Then they shade the expected range of the graph at the different time points so they can see who is falling below what is expected: who is out and who is in. Often they join the points for each individual so they can look at the different slopes to see rate of progress. A visual like this is a constant reminder of which students need particular attention with respect to pace of learning.

There is also the question of whether some aspects of learning are foundational, in that they need to be securely established in order to build new learning. You might need to find out how well students have mastered certain basic learning. For example, knowledge of spelling–sound correspondence is a prerequisite to using invented spelling to record ideas in writing. A basic sight word vocabulary leaves some cognitive capacity spare to work on figuring out unknown words in reading. If students have no schema for a narrative (that is, they don't know about the usual structure of a story), then they have no frame or scaffold that can help them process incoming information when reading or listening to a story.

Arguably, finding out where students are in order to move forward also entails

> Multiple sources of appropriate evidence (formal and informal) inform decisions about achievement and the nature of instruction.

being prepared to gather information about students' backgrounds and the resources they have for learning. These resources for learning include the features of their language(s) with which they are familiar and their knowledge of events that might provide the content for writing or the schema to aid comprehension. This information comes from a variety of sources, including evidence from ongoing participation in classroom activities, from parents and families and from other school sources (such as specialist teachers). Teachers have to learn about their students and their backgrounds in order to personalise instruction, something that is especially important in a classroom context with Māori and Pacific students (McNaughton, 2002).

Evaluating student learning in terms of where they are currently involves making informed choices about the means (tools and processes) of obtaining valid and systematic evidence of student learning profiles. Tools selected to assess student learning not only have to be sound (measure what they claim to in a reliable way) but also appropriate to the purpose; that is, they need to provide the right *sort* of information. If the purpose is to find out how well the students are doing relative to curriculum expectations then, clearly, the assessment tool(s) should be referenced to the curriculum. If the aim is to ascertain whether students have met a standard, then the means of assessment should provide information that relates to the criteria in the standard. This involves an understanding of the elements that comprise the standard.

The information obtained from one source should be cross-checked with that gleaned by other means. Often the information from a tool or test should be considered in the light of the bank of professional knowledge about students that teachers build through ongoing observation and interaction. Table 6.1 illustrates, at different levels, the characteristics of assessment as schools make increasingly effective choices regarding inquiry into student learning.

Table 6.1 A continuum of capability for assessing learning

	Basic	Mixed	Integrated
Selecting appropriate diagnostic measures to ascertain a pattern of achievement	There is one measure, used on one-off occasions, and the diagnostic information obtained is limited.	There is some evidence of cross-checking with more than one measure, and some diagnostic information is obtained at more than one point.	Triangulated achievement information is gathered, detailed diagnostic and curriculum-relevant information is obtained, progress-rate information is ascertained and tracking systems are in place.

Making an overall teacher judgement in relation to whether a student has met a particular standard involves a professional judgement, but one based on information gathered from a variety of sources, and these sources are likely to include both formal (standardised) and informal measures. Here is a good example of how this might operate.

CASE STUDY 6.1

The teachers in the junior syndicate were considering the new reading and writing standards for "after one year" at school. They unpacked the knowledge, skills and dispositions that seemed to be contained in the standard. Then, together, they identified how they could best obtain information about each student's performance in terms of the knowledge, skills and dispositions required. They consulted the Literacy Learning Progressions to work out what they should be "noticing" that would help indicate student understanding as they interacted with each student around text. They talked about what type of information they obtained from running records that would help them to see where a student was in relation to the reading standard. They looked at various examples of student writing at new entrant and Year 1 so that they could readily identify evidence of features that indicated the students were likely to be writing in a way that showed they met the standard. The teachers also compiled a series of questions or prompts they might use to ask students about their reading or writing that were likely to reveal student understanding or perhaps help students explain their understanding and use of strategy or process.

As part of the process of evaluating where students are at, manageable systems need to be devised for recording and monitoring the progress of students, including their progress over time. Although schools generally have systems (of varying degrees of utility) to record test data, these may need to be reconsidered in terms of recording information about attainment of standards. It would seem to be important to record not simply the final judgement but also the various measures and "noticings" that led to the judgement. These data should be organised in a logical, complete and systematic way, and the interpretations made from the data recorded and linked to them. There would need to be consistency across teachers at a given level in terms of a core set of ways and measures used to come to the judgement.

Both data and interpretations should be readily available at a classroom and a school level. This means that schools would need to have management systems capable of recording both numerical data and more qualitative data in the form of statements or comments. Full reporting to parents would seem to require an "audit trail" of evidence from various sources

> Systematically record the "audit trail" of evidence that informed a final judgement.

that were used to make the overall judgement. The interpretation of the information should be a shared task, and the inferences taken from the analyses should be agreed on by the appropriate group within the school community.

Partnerships in assessment for teaching and learning

Part of the process of evaluating student learning involves ensuring the students understand the desired outcomes. However, they also need to understand the *reasons* why these outcomes are important to them and where they are currently placed in relation to these outcomes. Finally, it should be made clear how a partnership will operate between the teacher and the students to ensure they achieve the desired outcomes.

> Ensure students understand the learning outcomes and the reasons they are valued.

The ongoing process of finding out about student learning is known as *assessment for learning*. A recent change within the broad strategy of assessment for learning is the shift in emphasis from the act of teaching to that of learning. While earlier work focused on teaching, and the role of teachers in gathering information and using it to inform and evaluate their teaching, assessment is being reframed as a social, collaborative activity, one that is aligned more with learning (Black & Wiliam, 2006). The spotlight has shifted to the teacher and the students working in partnership (Hawe, Dixon, & Watson, 2008) to ensure progress in learning. Students are being accorded a more significant role in their learning, and in the process of assessing such learning, with the aim of developing more self-regulated learners.

So, while teachers need to know their students, they also need to develop the capability to support and enable their students to self-evaluate and become self-regulating learners. In order to self-evaluate, students arguably need to understand learning goals and what a quality outcome, in terms of the goal or goals, might look like. In other words, they need the requisite criterion information against which to measure their learning to see if they have achieved the goal(s). Students also need to know where they are in relation to the desired outcome, and the steps they need to take to achieve it.

> Teachers actively support student self-evaluation as part of developing self-regulating learners.

To inquire into their own learning, students require support in terms of both this information about learning and also strategies to help them engage in self-evaluation. In our research in schooling improvement, both teachers and students report that students receive and have discussed with them the results from various assessments, and that they have occasional opportunities to "mark" or comment on the work of peers. The issue is, however, whether students have the opportunity to review their own work systematically, evaluate their learning *and* receive feedback on how well they are doing in such evaluation.

One of the best ways for students to understand what they are aiming towards is for there to be quite detailed discussion of exemplars. This involves deconstructing the features that contribute to exemplifying the required performance level. Students require extensive, carefully scaffolded practice at evaluation in much the same way as they require practice to participate effectively in peer collaborative discussions. They need to begin in a small way, with some quite specific evaluative task or tasks, then build. It would be unrealistic to present even a student-friendly form of an asTTle writing rubric (Glasswell, Parr, & Aikman, 2001) and expect students to be able to apply it to their own writing. However, one of the dimensions from the asTTle scoring rubric (e.g., structure) could be written in student-speak and examples at different levels of performance provided to help students see how the criteria can be applied to the samples of writing they and their peers produce. Remember that self-evaluation is more challenging than evaluating the performance of another.

The framework below (Table 6.2) shows what this process of supporting students to self-regulate their learning might look like, from an initial beginning to a high level of practice.

Note that if you as a teacher want to find out how you are going in terms of providing your students with the support and experience to allow them to self-evaluate, you could ask them to report the extent to which they feel they are prepared to engage in self-evaluation. This could be done by asking, orally, a series of simple questions, or asking for written ratings in response to a series of questions or statements similar to the ones we have used in our research (Timperley & Parr, 2009). The simple oral questions (and reasons for asking them) are along the lines of:

- What are you learning to do in [the subject] today? (to ascertain their understanding of learning goals)
- How do you know or work out what a good [outcome of what they are learning] looks like? (to ascertain their understanding of success criteria for performance)

Table 6.2 A continuum of capability for enabling student self-evaluation

	Basic	Mixed	Integrated
Student understanding of goals and their own learning	Learning goals are presented (along with success criteria). It is assumed that students understand what they are learning and what it will look like if achieved.	Students understand the reasons for specific learning, are able to work out some of their own learning goals and have a nonspecific understanding of what to do to reach more immediate goals.	Students are able (with support) to evaluate their own performance accurately, and they understand where they are in relation to desired quality performance (and the reasons for such goals) and what specifically is needed in order to reach them.
Student engagement in self-assessment	Students read over or check their own work, read/hear the work of others and comment or give a mark.	Students have checklist-like criteria to use in self- or peer assessment, and can identify where their performance can be improved. There is little checking of the accuracy of self-/peer assessment.	Students regularly self- and peer assess using clear, operationalised criteria/exemplars, and identify their performance level and where and how this can be improved. They are given feedback on the extent to which they do this accurately.

- Do you know how to work out how well you are going in [subject]? (to ascertain their understanding of their current level of performance)
- What do you have to do to improve? (to ascertain their understanding of how to close the gap between current and desired performance).

The written statements students rate are similar, starting with the stem "I know how to work out …", and concern how well they are going in a given curriculum area, what their learning goals are or what they are aiming to learn, what it would look like if they were to achieve a quality performance and what they have to do to achieve this (and how to do it). This type of probe of student preparedness to self-evaluate provides teachers with valuable information about the impact of their teaching.

Identifying professional learning needs in relation to student learning needs, and deciding on and taking appropriate action

There are two desirable responses to the information from any profile of student learning. One is to check what is known about the effectiveness of current classroom practice through ongoing inquiry. This involves systematic, evidence-informed inquiry to establish what has been effective, and with which students the practices are effective or not effective. The inquiry also has to offer explanations encompassing the likely reasons for differential effectiveness. In our research into schooling improvement, this area of systematically linking specific aspects of classroom practice to patterns of student achievement appears to be an area where more work is needed. In the Building Evaluative Capability Project, few schools could demonstrate that they were collecting evidence that would allow them to see how particular classroom practices that may have been the target of professional learning were being implemented, and how the nature and extent of that implementation was affecting student learning. In terms of the descriptors in Table 6.3, which outline the nature and extent of linking student achievement and classroom practice at varying levels of specificity, many schools were at a basic level.

> Check the effectiveness of current practices in relation to specific aspects of achievement profiles. Where a gap is apparent, source research evidence of effective practices relevant to the current context.

A second response (which appears in the mixed category of Table 6.3) should be to inquire into what have been demonstrably effective ways of addressing similar learning needs in similar contexts. This inquiry involves a careful consideration of sound research evidence about effective, high-leverage practices that are likely to be able to be applied in the present context. The practices need to have credibility in relation to the students, to the current nature of their achievement and to their rate of progress relative to that required (e.g., to reach curriculum expectations or attain valued outcomes). These two responses provide key information for formulating or revising a theory for improvement.

> Focus observations of practice on key aspects known to be important in relation to student learning needs.

When it is clear what the effective practices are, the inquiry should shift to a close look at the nature of the professional knowledge required in relation to the practices. In essence this professional knowledge comprises content knowledge about the subject (maths, or history, or reading) and pedagogical content knowledge (PCK)

Table 6.3 A continuum of capability for linking practice and student achievement data

	Basic	Mixed	Integrated
Use of student learning information to evaluate practice	Little or no connection is made between students' patterns of performance and classroom practices. (It may be informal statements, but there are no data on classroom practice that allow this link to be made.)	Data on practice are collected, but they cannot be specifically related to student achievement patterns. Practices applicable to meeting student needs are identified and implemented, but there is no systematic checking of the effects.	Current classroom practice is evaluated and links are established between practice and current patterns of achievement before identifying the changes needed. Changes are drawn from effective practice literature. Informed adaptation of practices is evident to increase effectiveness, and there is systematic checking of the effects.

that includes knowledge of the subject that is germane to teaching it (Shulman, 1987). This is the professional knowledge that needs to be acquired to address the gap between the current level and profile of achievement and the desired level and profile. Once it is established what teachers need to know in order to engage in these practices, then some form of stocktake is required to find out the current state of teacher knowledge and action with regard to them. Teacher learning, like student learning, should be tailored to need and circumstance.

Finding out about teacher content and PCK is not straightforward. Content knowledge is knowledge of the subject, while PCK is the particular way a teacher has to know the subject in order to teach it to others (Shulman, 1987). Knowledge is really important at a number of points in the inquiry cycle. A well-developed "theory of the task" (what is actually involved in the aspect of learning you are interested in assessing) is required to select an appropriate way to assess it (Timperley & Parr, 2004). Knowledge is important at the stage of interpreting student achievement data (as discussed in Chapter Eight). Research we have conducted (Parr & Timperley, 2008; Parr, 2009) shows very clearly that teachers can readily learn to interpret data accurately, but this is not what predicts whether their students will make progress. The all-important part is having sufficient PCK to apply the information gained about performance in order to work out the best way to move learning forward.

In one study we found that the capability of teachers to give the sort of written feedback to student writing that contains the hallmarks of high-quality formative feedback (feedback that helps students see where they are, what they are aiming for and how best to get there) predicted the extent of student progress in writing. The relationship between teacher PCK in this regard and progress was strong (Parr & Timperley, 2008). Writing is an area where teachers acquire considerable PCK from engaging in expertly facilitated collegial discussion around the moderation of writing (examples of building PCK in a professional learning community are outlined in Chapter Eight).

Although establishing teacher PCK is problematic, finding out about teaching practice would seem to be relatively straightforward: you simply observe the teacher in the classroom. However, in reality it is a complex process. An important consideration involves identifying the salient aspects of teaching that should be observed. What aspects of practice are the ones to focus on? Teaching practice includes, in broad terms, teaching moves such as interactions with students (particularly feedback and feedforward), modelling, explaining and other deliberate acts of teaching, deploying resources or artefacts and materials, aligning assignments and activities with learning aims and creating a supportive classroom environment. In many schools we have worked in, classroom observations are undertaken, but these are often linked to performance appraisals, or the teacher selects the focus according to personal professional learning goals. A major drawback to this is that the information about practice may not relate to the current focus in terms of student learning needs or the focus of professional learning, nor are the data necessarily collected in a systematic fashion. If teachers in a school syndicate or department are observed to have a variety of different focuses, there is no opportunity to aggregate and consider the resulting pattern in relation to student achievement and the professional learning they have engaged in. The aim should be to focus on observing those aspects of practice that have been shown to be most likely to lead to improvement in the areas of student learning identified as requiring attention—the aspects of practice that are to be worked on or that are being developed.

Obtaining valid and systematic information about these selected aspects of practice involves operationalising key relevant aspects of practice; that is, defining in detail what is to be observed, or what the concept looks like in practice (e.g., what does quality feedback look like?). Suitable tools need to be used, both to focus the observation and to help evaluate the practice. The tool might be derived from descriptions of effective practice as defined in the research literature, but it should be used to help develop among teachers a shared understanding of practice. Spillane and colleagues (2002) define tools in this context as externalised representations of ideas that people use in their practice. To qualify as a "smart tool" (Robinson, Hōhepa, & Lloyd, 2009) there are two main requirements: the ideas represented in the tool have to be valid (e.g., represent accepted dimensions of effective practice), and the ideas must be represented in a quality way. For an observation tool, a quality way would mean a way that allows it to serve as an indicator of the nature of such practice. In terms of the quality of the ideas the tool represents, these authors suggest that smart tools incorporate sound theory about how to achieve the purpose of the task in question.

An example of this specifying in detail what the concept looks like in practice is illustrated here using a tool devised to observe literacy practice (Parr & Hawe, 2008). This tool was designed in collaboration with teachers in two schools. Together we drew on the effective practice literature related to literacy and our collective experience. We drafted and tested the elements and descriptors in the tool, paying particular attention to whether they described observable practice in a way that allowed it to be reliably evaluated. Later, the teachers in a third school, who were observing one another teaching using a version of this tool, were having difficulty knowing what effective feedback might look like. We revised the tool once again, made the descriptors of practice more specific (see Table 6.4) and in workshops used examples from transcripts of actual practice to help them see what different types and levels of feedback looked like.

Although the tool and the associated examples may help to specify what the practice actually looks like and to build knowledge, in most instances it is not the tool itself that promotes the learning. Rather, it is how the tool is integrated into the routines of practice that promotes learning. For example, it may be the act of observing others and having to think about the observed practice in relation to ideal practice, then articulating the perceived gap in order to provide feedback to the teacher observed, that actually stimulates the greatest learning.

A valid and reliable evaluation of practice also involves repeated observations, as studies of school instruction typically show large variations in each teacher's

Table 6.4 Progression re quality of feedback to students' productive activity during literacy

Quality of achievement-related feedback				COMMENTS / EVIDENCE
Teacher's feedback is not directly related to achievement (rather it is approving, rewarding, disapproving of behaviour).	Teacher's feedback refers in a general manner to: success criteria ☐ generic aspects of literacy learning ☐.	Teacher tells the learner about **whether** their work has met / has not met: success criteria ☐ generic aspects of literacy learning ☐.	Teacher tells the learner about **how** their work has met / has not met: success criteria ☐ generic aspects of literacy learning ☐.	
Quality of improvement-related feedback				
Teacher provides feedback regarding aspects to improve, but these are not directly related to the success criteria or learning aim.	Teacher's feedback makes no direct reference to what needs improvement and how to go about improvement, rather it refers in general manner to: success criteria ☐ generic aspects of literacy learning ☐.	Teacher tells the learner about **what** needs to be improved, with reference to: success criteria ☐ generic aspects of literacy learning ☐.	Teacher tells the learner about **how** to improve their work, with reference to: success criteria ☐ generic aspects of literacy learning ☐.	

Source: Parr and Hawe (2008).
Note that although this tool was designed to be applied to literacy practice, it could be readily adapted to other curriculum areas.

practices over time as well as substantial variation among teachers—even those at the same year level in the same school. The number of samples needed for reliable and valid representations of practice has been placed at between six and eight (Croninger & Valli, 2009). Observation of practice is a time-consuming and resource-intensive process, so doing this number of samples is not practical in a school unless the observations are spread over quite some time. However, the message regarding the effort needed to ensure reliable and valid information is important.

The evidence from observations, particularly if they are more than just a snapshot, should be triangulated with other sources of information about practice. This additional information might be in documents such as lesson or unit plans, and assignments set for students (both the nature of the assignment and samples of work). It might also come from practice that is reported by the teachers themselves, who present evidence to support their descriptions. Schools need to find ways to record the nature of the specific elements of practice observed so that they can track them over time and link the patterns they find to the professional learning undertaken, and to student learning. In the example above (see Table 6.4), the teacher's practice regarding feedback was categorised in one of a series of three ordinal categories. Ordinal categories specify an order, in this case increasing levels of effectiveness of practice (regarding achievement and improvement-related feedback). As a result, a school is able to see where each teacher is and use this information, and the pattern across teachers, to plan professional learning. Later, repeat observations to see if teachers have moved up categories, help to evaluate the success of this professional learning.

Observers of classroom practice have to possess considerable PCK and skill, both to know what they are looking for and to provide feedback to the teacher observed (Timperley & Parr, 2008). Without this skill, the risk is that "change" messages will not be given in such a way that they are heard. There is potential for valuable additional learning from engaging in peer observations (Parr & Hawe, 2009), or shared observations such as those entailed in "lesson study" approaches, where groups of teachers engage in joint observation, analysis and evaluation of lessons (Darling-Hammond & Bransford, 2005). The additional value of these approaches is that shared knowledge may contribute to greater coherence in practice. In very successful schooling improvement models, the wide variation in practice among teachers—and within the same teacher at different times and in different contexts—is reduced (Croninger & Valli, 2009; Rowan & Correnti, 2009). Coherence in teaching practices within a school has been linked to greater effectiveness.

Once the nature of current practice has been captured, the likely high-leverage practice with respect to student learning needs has been identified from research and professional expertise, and an indication has been obtained of teachers' content and pedagogical content knowledge and skill in relation to such practice, then planning and implementing the necessary professional learning can begin. The choice of how that learning is obtained is vital. The major response to learning is action undertaken in the classroom—action that is appropriately supported and monitored.

As already mentioned, an important part of these practices should be to ensure the involvement of students in their own learning. This involves the source of information about learning and achievement moving from feedback provided *to* the student, to information generated *by* the student. Through their actions in sharing their professional knowledge with their students, teachers should be ensuring that students have the knowledge and skills necessary to inquire into their own learning and become self-monitoring (to evaluate strengths and weaknesses and to make appropriate decisions about action, including where to obtain support and how to formulate future goals). This involves teachers making explicit the professional knowledge they may hold implicitly, such as what makes for a good piece of writing or the strategies that good readers use. Quality feedback is the vital ingredient, and the degree and nature of the teacher's control over the feedback process is important. Practices such as appraising your own work and that of your peers are a way for students to develop such productive knowledge and expertise. Part of the evaluation of classroom practice should include an inquiry into the extent to which students display this knowledge and these behaviours.

As mentioned above, we have found that a few quite simple questions asked of students helped teachers to gauge how well they were preparing students to engage in self-evaluation. Clearly there are other indicators as well, including student responses in classroom interactions with their teacher and peers, and the visible products of their learning (worked examples, writing samples, etc.).

Monitoring effectiveness of action in relation to its impact on valued outcomes

When a course of action in relation to practice is undertaken, it needs to be evaluated in an ongoing way. Its effect on individual students—and sometimes groups of students where there is a shared learning need (such as students with English as an additional language)—has to be tracked. This reflects the cyclical, ongoing nature of assessment for learning. Evidence of learning—or, more specifically, evidence of gaps in learning—leads to adjustments in practice, further assessment and then, where required, readjustment of practice.

Re-engaging in the cycle

Inquiry is a recursive process. Current or new learning is incorporated into a new cycle of inquiry and knowledge building. This essentially requires self-regulation on the part of teachers. Self-regulation involves teachers being able to evaluate the effect of their own practice on students (to continue to evaluate their own strengths and weaknesses in relation to the outcomes of an evaluation of student learning profiles; and to make appropriate decisions about action, including where to obtain support and how to formulate future goals). Re-engagement in the cycle of inquiry may involve a more specific focus or further adaptation. A teacher engaged in ongoing inquiry is engaged in a process critical to their role as adaptive expert.

Even in the classrooms of teachers whose students, on average, make good progress, there are those students who do not. For these students, the identified, high-leverage practices engaged in have not been effective. Such a situation sometimes involves a considered decision by the teacher to give the current practices a little longer, or a little more emphasis. However, it is preferable that they engage in identifying what might be termed *next practice* (Hannon, 2009). This involves recontextualising and reformulating the practice, and thinking laterally and problem solving what might work for those students in the current context. Next practice is likely to take teachers well out of their comfort zones and may involve using previously untried media for learning.

Reflection questions

QUESTION 1

Using the descriptors in Tables 6.1, 6.2 and 6.3, take each table in turn and decide where your school is currently placed in relation to:

a. Assessing learning

BASIC	MIDDLE/MIXED	INTEGRATED

b. Enabling student self-evaluation

BASIC	MIDDLE/MIXED	INTEGRATED

c. Linking student achievement and classroom practice

BASIC	MIDDLE/MIXED	INTEGRATED

QUESTION 2

What is the evidence for deciding the school is basic, mixed or integrated in each case?

a. Assessing learning

BASIC	MIDDLE/MIXED	INTEGRATED

b. Enabling student self-evaluation

BASIC	MIDDLE/MIXED	INTEGRATED

c. Linking student achievement and classroom practice

BASIC	MIDDLE/MIXED	INTEGRATED

QUESTION 3

What is the way forward (consider priorities, key levers) for the school in order to progress, in terms of evaluative capability in each of these three areas?

References

Black, P., & Wiliam, D. (2006). Developing a theory of formative assessment. In J. Gardner (Ed.), *Assessment and learning* (pp. 81–100). London: Sage.

Croninger, R. G., & Valli, L. (2009). "Where is the action?" Challenges to studying the teaching of reading in elementary classrooms. *Educational Researcher, 38*(2), 100–108.

Darling-Hammond, L., & Bransford, J. (Eds.). (2005). *Preparing teachers for a changing world.* San Francisco: John Wiley.

Glasswell, K., Parr, J. M., & Aikman, M. (2001). *Development of the asTTle writing assessment rubrics for scoring extended writing tasks.* asTTle Technical Report 26. Wellington: Ministry of Education; Auckland: The University of Auckland.

Hannon, V. (2009, January). *Keynote address.* Presented at the International Congress for Schooling Effectiveness and Improvement, Vancouver, Canada.

Hawe, E., Dixon, H., & Watson, E. (2008). Oral feedback in the context of written language. *Australian Journal of Language and Literacy, 31,* 43–58.

McNaughton, S. (2002). *Meeting of minds.* Wellington: Learning Media.

Parr, J. M. (2009, July). *Building professional knowledge to teach writing.* Paper presented at the United Kingdom Literacy Association 45th annual conference, Greenwich, London.

Parr, J. M., & Hawe, E. (2008). *Measuring classroom literacy practice.* Final report of a Teaching and Learning Research Initiative. Available at www.tlri.org.nz

Parr, J. M., & Timperley, H. (2008). Teachers, schools and using evidence: considerations of preparedness. *Assessment in Education, 15*(1), 57–71.

Parr, J. M., & Timperley, H. (in press). *Feedback to writing, assessment for teaching and learning and student progress.*

Robinson, V., Hōhepa, M., & Lloyd, C. (2009). *School leadership and student outcomes: Identifying what works and why: Best evidence synthesis iteration.* Wellington: Ministry of Education.

Rowan, B., & Correnti, R. (2009). Studying reading instruction with teacher logs: Lessons from the study of instructional improvement. *Educational Researcher, 38*(2), 120–131.

Shulman, L. S. (1987). Knowledge and teaching: Foundations of the new reform. *Harvard Educational Review, 57,* 1–22.

Spillane, J. P., Reiser, B. J., & Reimer, T. (2002). Policy implementation and cognition: Reframing and refocusing implementation research. *Review of Educational Research, 72,* 387–431.

Timperley, H. S., & Parr, J. M. (2004). *Using evidence in teaching practice: Implications for professional learning.* Auckland: Hodder-Moa-Beckett.

Timperley, H., & Parr, J. M. (2008, September*). Facilitation and feedback.* Paper presented to the British Educational Research Association conference, Edinburgh.

Timperley, H. S., & Parr, J. M. (2009). What is this lesson about? Instructional processes and student understandings in the writing classroom. *The Curriculum Journal, 20*(1), 43–60.

7

Ensuring Quality Evidence of Student Achievement to use for Improvement

Rachel Dingle and Judy Parr

In this book we have focused on inquiry into practice. The key inquiry concerns whether practice is enhancing student learning and achievement. This chapter is concerned with measures of student achievement. It looks at how schools can ensure they collect, store and analyse quality student achievement data. Schools need these quality data for two main reasons. One is diagnostic and development-focused, to find out about students' strengths and learning needs in order to help develop appropriate teaching programmes. The other is evaluative, to find out how effective the programmes or changes to teaching practice have been at various levels in a school (class, year and whole school) or for different groups of students.

Quality data are data that can be trusted, but they are also data that give information about what teachers and leaders are specifically interested in finding out about (like reading for meaning, or computation using fractions), and which is the main reason for collecting those data. These quality data form the basis for inquiring into understanding what needs to change to make a difference to student learning, and later to check whether everyone's improvement efforts have been successful. The ability to gather and use this evidence, and to know what actions to take and how to evaluate them, is part of the continuing cycle of inquiry.

From our experience we know there are systems and processes in place in nearly all schools to collect and record student achievement data and for checking the accuracy of these data for a single time-point assessment. However, not all schools have the capability to store and analyse data in a way that allows the progress of individual students over time to be measured. This is necessary to inform judgements relating to progression towards, for example, a standard. Also, schools may have been largely storing information from only one measure, yet teachers will use multiple sources of evidence to make their overall judgement as to whether a student has met a particular standard of achievement. Although this range of sources of evidence will usually include one or two test-like measures, it is likely that schools will want to think about how to enter and store systematically the results from at least some of the other sources that informed the teacher judgement.

> Plan a system that will hold records of a test conducted at several time points and will allow information from more than one type of measure to be recorded against each individual student.

This chapter is designed to help schools to collect, store and analyse quality data in order to strengthen their ability to inquire into their practice, particularly in terms of informed judgements about student achievement and progress. Some of the language used may be unfamiliar, and so as an aid to understanding there is a glossary of statistical terms at the end of the chapter.

Why collect data?

What evidence is needed in terms of student learning depends on the particular reason, the *why*, for collecting it. The use to which the data are to be put determines what data collected and how they are collected. There should be as much time spent planning what data to collect to answer inquiry questions, and how to obtain these data, as is spent later analysing and making sense of the data.

In many cases the purpose of assessment is formative, to guide day-to-day decisions about instruction in classrooms, and much assessment is done by the teacher in the course of ongoing observations and conversations. This process is termed *interactive formative* assessment (Cowie & Bell, 1999) and is often stored as a mental note in the teacher's "log-in-the-head", or in physical notes (actual log entries). However, sometimes the diagnostic purpose is more formal and takes the form of planned formative assessment (Cowie & Bell, 1999) to establish student patterns of strengths and gaps in learning across a class or school. Clearly, the tool selected has to provide suitable

> Be clear about the purpose for collecting data— the questions the data are intended to answer.

diagnostic information and, where appropriate, diagnostic information that relates to the curriculum and the teaching that has gone on.

An equally important reason to collect student achievement evidence is to see how students are performing: to ascertain what level of achievement they have reached and how this stacks up relative to students in other, similar schools, or in comparison to the average student nationally. At other times the reason is specifically to inquire into the rate of progress to see where there are gains over time, and to see whether students have accelerated or reached a plateau.

Measuring level of achievement and progress

When attempting to ascertain a student's level of achievement and their achievement relative to others, and to gauge their progress, it is important to:
- make sure that each measure is administered in an appropriate and consistent manner (across contexts and time)
- use a range of measures, including nationally standardised assessments.

Why is it important to administer each test consistently? If the conditions are pretty much the same each time and for everyone who sits the test, it gives schools more confidence when comparing their students with others, and when measuring progress it helps ensure that like are being compared with like.

Why include standardised tests? These provide the yardstick by which to judge a school's efforts. The use of nationally standardised tests allows teachers and leaders to compare the level attained, or the progress they have measured in their students, with the expected level or average gain for that group of students. The yardstick allows them to tell how much more than expected the students' gains were, and this information is a very important basis on which to judge efforts, particularly for those students who are well below the cohort. Teachers and leaders can see whether they have accelerated the pace of progress over time. They also know whether any progress being made is real or just "chance", because tests give the measurement error. For example, in asTTle the error of measurement is 15 points, so if students are within 15 points of one another, or a group of students gains less than 15 points, to all intents and purposes they have performed the same.

- Use measures consistently.
- Include standardised measures.
- Use a range of measures.

Why a range of measures? Schools need a range of measures for three reasons. For one thing, with a range a teacher does not have to rely on a single occasion to assess the performance of the student, so is likely to obtain a more complete and potentially fairer picture of performance. Multiple sources of evidence also allow teachers to gain different information, and a richer picture of performance, because different ways of assessing something are not likely to be measuring a construct in the same way. More than one measure allows teachers to check what one measure tells them against the information from another. Different means of obtaining information (student work samples, observations, questioning, etc.) inform teacher professional judgement. In a standards environment, the notion of overall teacher judgement is premised on the use of a number of sources of evidence.

However, it is important to realise that different tests or measures cannot necessarily be compared directly. This is because of the very fact that they are *different* measures of a construct. A useful analogy is to think of measuring student fitness based on the time taken to complete an activity. Suppose that some schools decide to measure the time their students take to swim 100 metres, some measure the time taken to run 500 metres and others measure the time taken to cycle five kilometres. All would be valid measures of fitness, all could potentially be used to measure improvement in fitness, but none could be compared directly. So a school could not use swimming in February to measure fitness, then running in August (when it is too cold to swim in the outdoor pool!). The school has to use the same measure at a later time to gauge progress.

But even the same test cannot be compared at times because the tests may have been taken under quite different conditions. Suppose that the schools using swimming to test fitness used a variety of kinds of pool: some were salt water, some fresh water and some of the fresh-water pools were heated to a constant temperature while others were unheated outdoor pools. Some may even have timed students swimming in open water (sea or lake). These swimming conditions are not comparable, so it is not possible to compare schools. Likewise, cycling times in a place that has hills and gusty winds might prove more variable than those where the terrain is flat and the wind light. If all the running were to be done around a sheltered sports field, those times would be the most reliable (in both the lay and statistical sense of the word) and comparable.

However, if measuring students' all-round fitness is what is needed, then measuring their running and swimming and cycling rates would give a more complete picture than any one measurement on its own; it is the idea of using a range to measure the concept (in this case, fitness). A school may use a range of tests to allow them to measure different aspects of an overall construct in the most appropriate way. For example, oracy, reading, spelling and writing all contribute to an overall measure of literacy, but they require different tests. In the same content area, such as reading, teachers and their leaders can look at results on different tests, both formal and informal, to triangulate (or check) their findings. If two tests of reading, for example, or one test and a more informal check, such as a student's current book level, give very different measures of progress, then the teacher would stop and reflect. They would need to think about exactly what they are measuring, whether they are using appropriate tools, and the strengths and weaknesses, as tested, of a particular student (or group of students). Conversely, if two tests, or a test and a more informal measure, of a particular content area give similar pictures, they can be more confident in their findings (and their measures).

In order to measure progress, a school must use the same measure (or parallel versions of it) at two different times; for example, at the start and end of the year. If the school does not use the same measure, they cannot judge whether progress has actually been made. This is because if they use a different assessment tool from the first time, the reliability of the measure of progress is too low because of the potentially different focuses of the two tools. For example, a teacher cannot combine a student's Supplementary Tests of Achievement in Reading (STAR) score at the beginning of the year with their Assessment Tools for Teaching and Learning (asTTle) reading score at the end of a year. We have found that some schools have changed the assessment tool they were using between time points, either because they saw that another assessment tool offered advantages over the one they used initially, or because they changed the focus of an initiative they were engaged in. This means comparisons cannot be made. A school can, however, compare rates of progress of a group of students taking Reading Test Y at both time points with a group who took a different test, Reading Test Z, at both time points (see the section "Measuring the amount of change", p. 141).).

In order to compare the rate of progress of students to expected progress (that is, the average progress nationally for that group), schools need to use a standardised measure that has national norms. They cannot, for example, consider their students' progress against expected progress using the national writing exemplars. This tool allows a school to ascertain a level for their writers, and even to track how many sublevels students progress in a given time period. But the school cannot say whether this is at, above or below average, because there are no norms derived from a large representative sample to compare against.

SUMMARY SO FAR

- Use assessment tools that measure the valued outcome(s) aimed for and that are able to provide the information to answer a particular inquiry.
- Use nationally standardised tests to measure achievement level relative to expectations, and to measure rate of progress.
- Use a range of measures to gain a richer, more reliable picture of learning.
- Use each measure in a consistent way, across time and contexts.

Data collection and scoring

There are a number of steps to consider under the broad heading of data collection. As we mentioned above, it is important that any measure is administered appropriately and consistently. It is also important to ensure the measure is scored reliably. Finally, all data have to be recorded and stored accurately.

Part of assuring quality data where there are open-ended responses or assessments subject to interpretation, such as writing samples, is to agree on the

- Score reliably.
- Moderate scoring.
- Record accurately.
- Record details in full.

score or level. Everyone needs to have a shared understanding of the application of the criteria for marking so that students are marked fairly and reliably. This understanding should not only be shared among teachers in a school: the understanding should align closely with expert views or exemplars. After all, the teachers in a syndicate in a school could agree on a level for a piece of writing but still be inaccurate in relation to an established standard—they could all be marking higher or lower. This consistency is important when considering the scores in relation to national normative data. Moderation processes have to be put in place to ensure there is agreement on the meaning of criteria, there is agreement on what criteria at different levels look like in practice (in a writing sample, for instance) and there are procedures to check for differences in scoring. These moderation processes cannot be confined to a school or group of teachers. They must be in reference to an external, agreed standard.

In recording the information from tests and other assessments, planning is required to set up the database in a way that allows the answers to be obtained to the particular questions we want answered. In order to measure progress, schools need to be able to match an individual's score at different points in time. Thus, the test score needs to be stored alongside important demographic variables such as age, date of birth, gender and ethnicity that identify a unique individual. A school may also want to use these variables in analysis to answer questions such as whether boys are achieving as well as girls, or questions concerning age-related trends in the data. Other helpful information to collect, depending on the nature of the inquiries planned, might be English as a Second Language (ESOL) identification or learning-support identification (and perhaps the amount of time spent in either of these programmes, or year and month of entry to the programme). These variables would allow analysis at an individual level, by classroom, at a whole-school level or by specified group. The variables are best extracted or exported from the school management system (SMS), because they are then most likely to be correct, consistent and up to date.

A school is likely to use the student assessment data for both school- and year- or classroom-level planning, as well as for calculating summative level of achievement, how much progress has been made and impact measures (how much difference the school has made—how much "value" they have added), so all of the available information should be stored. In the case of a test that has multiple parts or dimensions, the subtest information as well as the total, scale and stanine scores should be recorded. The date of the assessment should also be included (the latter serves to double-check that the correct file is being used in conducting analyses). Part of the initial planning for data collection involves considering what factors teachers and leaders might want to look at that might explain the pattern of student achievement. If the intention is to analyse systematically classroom practice as well as student data, and to look for any relationships between the two, it would be wise to ensure this link is possible. Therefore, alongside student achievement data would be teacher name and perhaps other information, like number of years of teaching experience, or years at the particular school, or type and extent of professional development undertaken. Likewise, if a school wants to see whether particular student factors relate to achievement patterns, data such as the number of years the student has been at the school, whether s/he has left the school and returned (particularly if this happened more than once) or whether attendance is related to progress should be recorded for each student.

The data entered should be checked systematically for accuracy. Any instances of missing data should be examined to ensure that a correct identifier is used if the student was absent, so that it cannot be confounded with a nil score on the test. Also, it is often useful to be able to check whether those students who did not sit a test at a second or subsequent time were any different in performance initially from those students who stayed the distance. Otherwise progress could be explained, at least in part, by the fact that the lowest performing students left the school or class.

SUMMARY SO FAR

- Systematically check the accuracy of information.
- Extract or export student demographics from the SMS, where possible.
- Include *all* information from the assessment (e.g., date of test and test results, recorded at subtest or item level).
- Plan what information about teachers and/or students needs to be included to widen the potential analyses and the questions that can be answered.

Analysing and interpreting data

Five aspects of analysing and interpreting data are discussed below:
- understanding the current pattern of performance
- measuring progress
- tracking the rate of progress
- analysis of groups
- measuring the amount of change.

Understanding the current pattern of performance

Understanding patterns of performance involves diagnosing the pattern of strengths and gaps in order to build on what has been grasped and ascertain the direction in which to move learning forward. This analysis might include consideration of the pattern of errors or misconceptions. It also involves understanding where students are currently in relation to an agreed reference point, usually an external reference point such as a curriculum level, a standard or other national norm.

This relation is expressed in different ways. For example, it may involve a comparison of means. Table 7.1 is an example of using means (and standard deviations to give an idea of the extent to which scores vary around this mean) to compare the performance of boys and girls in each year level in relation to the national mean.

Table 7.1 Mean score for each year level, by gender

	Girls			Boys			National
Year	N	Mean score	SD	N	Mean score	SD	expected
4	104	433	78	98	405	81	412
5	75	466	69	76	444	77	462
6	101	501	84	95	475	84	489
7	105	585	72	110	569	74	508
8	102	613	74	103	582	74	517
9	96	634	125	83	585	116	634
10	106	652	135	119	612	120	728

Notes: N = number; SD = standard deviation.

Or, it may involve considering the percentage of students scoring at or above a certain point or standard. Table 7.2 shows the percentage of students in particular groups within a school who are at or above a certain target standard the school has set.

Analyses might include:
• level of performance
• relative level of performance
• patterns in performance
• progress (amount and rate).

Table 7.2 Percentage of students below, at or above standard, by ethnicity

Level	Māori %	Pacific %	NZE %	Expected %
Low	5	6	2	4
Below	44	53	34	36
At	15	13	19	20
Above	31	28	36	36
High	5	0	9	4

Note: NZE = New Zealand European.

Finally, to get an idea about relative performance—in this case performance compared to the national average performance across age or year groups—a visual can show a comparison of the distribution of scores or stanines to the normative distribution. Figure 7.1 illustrates the distribution of stanine scores on the STAR test relative to a normal distribution for a school at time 1 and then again at time 2 (after they have engaged in professional learning).

Figure 7.1 Percentage of students in each stanine at time 1 and time 2 relative to normative distribution

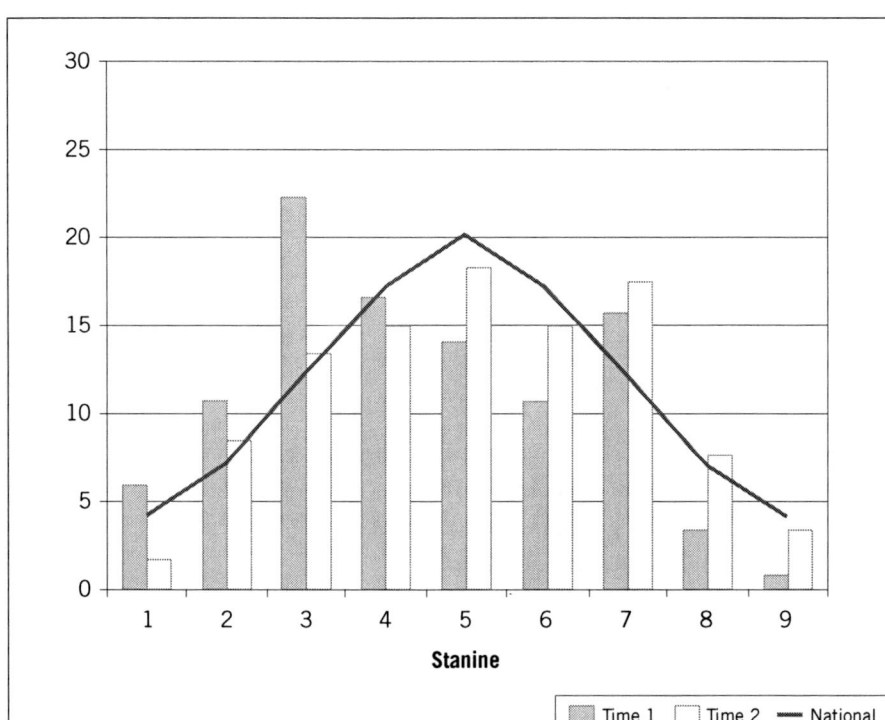

Measuring progress

Schools and teachers are mainly interested in how much they have managed to raise student achievement. They want to get a good indication of ongoing and future work and about what actions made the most impact. This latter inquiry involves linking achievement information to specific aspects of classroom and school programmes. The only way that progress can be measured, and therefore the impact of teachers' and leaders' work assessed, is by storing data about student achievement to allow individual students to be matched over time in a longitudinal analysis. Obviously, student data can be stored for one year and compared at the start and end of that year, but it is useful to store student data for longer periods and track students across year levels. This allows a school to see how long it takes them as a school to "get traction" in terms of accelerating progress. Most SMS in schools do not easily store data for longitudinal analysis, so it may be necessary to create a database to do this. This can be done in a variety of ways, depending on the resources and skills available in each school, or group of schools if working together. If a school regularly uses MS Excel (or a similar spreadsheet package), or MS Access (or a similar database package), then it is sensible to use one of these to store the data.[4]

There are some do's and don'ts around collecting and storing data for longitudinal analyses. Tracking students across years can be difficult if variations on the students' names are used at different times. An ID number is an alternative. Although some schools use an internal school ID number for their students, these are not necessarily helpful, because it would seem they can change with changing SMS system, installing upgrades or other improvements in process. The use of correctly recorded National Student Numbers (NSNs) would make matching data for individual students much easier.

The Dos:
- Record student names in full: surname and all first names.
- Take real care with hyphens, spaces and apostrophes (e.g., in Pacific names).
- Include date of birth.
- Follow the Ministry of Education conventions for recording ethnicity.
- Backup any ID number like the NSN with name and date of birth.

Measuring progress can be as simple as calculating the difference between two test scores assessed at different times. However, in order to calculate actual progress, teachers and leaders need to take into account how much progress is normally expected of a student as s/he matures. All published nationally standardised tests in New Zealand incorporate expected progress. This is the amount of gain each student is expected to make in the normal course of things, as they mature from one time point to the next. For example, published normative data show that between Years 4 and 6 a student is expected to make a gain of 100 points on a test just by being two years older. That is, on average, students make a gain of 100 points in two years. So, if a particular student actually makes 150 points' progress, then the actual or real progress made by that student is 50 points. This measure of expected gain is determined by the average gain made by New Zealand students over the time period being measured and is published as part of the assessment tool manual.

---

4 New generations of SMS software are planned to provide this capability.

There are typically two types of expected progress. One is the actual number of raw score points (score) a student is expected to gain on average between two time points (e.g., in asTTle or PAT). The second involves the use of a standardised measure, such as stanines (e.g., STAR). In this case, expected progress is somewhat different in that it is taken into account when converting a raw score to a stanine. A stanine score indicates how a student's achievement compares to his/her peers nationally. If a student remains in the same standardised band or grouping, s/he continues to have the same achievement level relative to others. Examples of these different types of expected progress are described below.

AsTTle has tests for Years 4–12. There are separate tests for writing, reading and mathematics, each measured on its own scale. These three scales cannot be compared directly. However, because each test is already measured on a single scale, comparisons can be made between students in different year levels, although each year has a different amount of expected progress. For example, the mean score, nationally, in Year 5 for asTTle reading is 462, and the mean score on the same test in Year 6 is 489. Expected progress (calculated from average gains nationally) is 27 points on the asTTle reading scale over the year. Therefore, a student gaining more than 27 points from Year 5 to Year 6 has progressed more than expected (compared to the average gain of New Zealand students).

The PATs are similar to asTTle in that they range from Year 4 to Year 10. Each year has a different amount of expected progress, and each subject test has its own scale, and so tests cannot be compared directly. For example, the mean score, nationally, in Year 5 for PAT mathematics, is 40.3, and the mean score on the same test in Year 6 is 46.4. Expected progress is then a gain of 6.1 on the PAT mathematics scale over the year. Therefore, a student gaining more than 6.1 from Year 5 to Year 6 has progressed more than expected (compared to the average gain of New Zealand students).

STAR has tests for Years 3–9. There are separate tests for Year 3, Years 4–6 and Years 7–9. The possible maximum score on each test version increases from 45 (Year 3) to 50 at Years 4–6, and then up to 80 for Years 7–9. These jumps in possible total raw score mean that raw scores from different year levels cannot be combined meaningfully. However, comparisons of performance or progress between students in different year levels can be made using stanines, because all stanine scores have a mean of 5 and standard deviation of 2. If a student is progressing at the same rate as they have so far (relative to their peers nationally), then they will score more marks (raw score) at each year level, but these gains will translate into the same stanine at each year level. For example, a student scoring 23 at the end of Year 4 and 28 at the end of Year 5 has continued to progress at the same rate and would be in stanine 4 at both time points. This means that a student who makes any stanine gain, for example, from stanine 4 at the end of Year 5 to stanine 5 at the end of Year 6, has progressed at more than his/her previous rate of progress, relative to his/her peers nationally.

Tracking the rate of progress

It is important to track the progress in student achievement over time because it allows a school to gauge whether the effects of any intervention are cumulative. Often the effect does not show in the early part of an intervention, and it is only by following progress over time that it can be seen.

Gains in achievement and gains made over a particular period of time may be insufficient for students to meet set targets or standards. Take a hypothetical Year 5 student, James, who has a below-average score at the beginning of the year and then gains the average 27 points. He is still below average. Although James has improved his own personal average amount of gain, in that this rate is now comparable to his peers, and although he has not fallen further behind, greater than average progress is needed for him to catch up to reach his expected level of performance in reading. As a result, schools often aim to accelerate the progress of their students beyond the average rate of improvement so that some students make progress sufficient to allow them to catch up and "close the gap" between themselves and those students who perform at or above a nationally expected level. How much acceleration is needed varies across and within schools.

Sometimes schools set targets that aim to move the current school average score from below the national average to at or above what is expected nationally. However, it should be kept in mind that this can be achieved while the performance of the large majority of students is still below that expected. This happens because students in one achievement band make all the gains—and make large gains. A more equitable target may be to move the whole distribution of scores towards the national distribution. This would mean that the target requires that all students move, some more than others, to reach the expected distribution. It is important to consider the whole distribution because often it is necessary to move the lowest achieving students at a more accelerated rate than the students towards the centre of the distribution. When aiming to do this, don't forget the highest achieving students: they need to be achieving at least at the same level as before, if not doing even better.

Analysis of groups

A school often wants to analyse the level of achievement or rate of progress of different groups within the student population. For example, a school may want to know: Are boys doing as well as girls? Is there a year group that does not achieve as well as the others? Do the lowest achieving students at the beginning of the year (say, the lowest 20 percent) make as much progress as the remaining 80 percent? These are often very useful analyses to do, because they can help with planning and assessing the impact of any new teaching interventions. When comparing groups it is important to look at averages and their variance—the amount of spread there is for each distribution. There are different ways to do this, including interpreting a mean and its standard deviation and looking at bar charts of distributions.

Care should be taken to ensure the groups being compared are large enough to be sure any patterns and trends shown are not just because of one particular teacher, or an atypical cohort of students or some other chance circumstance. A general rule of thumb is that if each group has 100 students or more, then a school can be fairly certain the differences seen are real—not just chance. Any groups smaller than 10 students are definitely too small to say anything meaningful about, and groups with fewer than 50 students may give misleading results (but it is impossible to know when this happens). So if a school is quite small, don't be surprised if there is a lot of variation in student achievement from year to year.

There is one other issue to consider when examining differences between groups. This occurs when a cohort of students is split into groups based on achievement; for example, to compare the lowest 20 percent of the cohort with the rest to see if they progress at different rates. The second and any subsequent assessments of these students will display something called "regression to the mean". Regression to the mean occurs whenever an extreme subset of individuals is selected (e.g., the lowest or highest 20 percent, based on their test scores at the first time of testing), and is then measured again on a second occasion. If the lowest achieving subset is selected, some of the individuals will have been included in the group because they achieved lower-than-average scores, but this was not a true reflection of their normal achievement

> When analysing groups, consider the size of the group, variability and regression to the mean.

level and so in the next test their scores are likely to be higher, or closer to their "true ability". The result is that the mean scores of the group on a second occasion will be higher, irrespective of anything else that happens between the tests. The same is true for the highest performing subset. In a second test, the mean for the group will be lower, as some individuals (those included in the group as the result of chance high scores) are likely to have lower scores than in the first test.

There are sophisticated calculations that can estimate the effect of regression to the mean based on how reliable the assessment tool is, among other things. However, making such calculations is not necessary most of the time. The salient point to take from this is that regression to the mean occurs, and that any differences you see between achievement groups should be treated with caution and an allowance made for the fact that some of that difference is due to this phenomenon.

Measuring the amount of change

There are a number of ways to measure the size of a change in achievement. As mentioned above, some measures show the amount of change over and above what is expected. But sometimes a school wants to compare measures of progress where different tools have been used. For example, they may want to see if progress in maths is greater than that in reading, but the different measures mean it is not simply a matter of comparing scores or means. Or even within reading, a school may use STAR at junior levels and asTTle:Reading at upper year levels, and these are not directly comparable, even though each is a measure of reading.

Effect size measures are useful to make comparisons of rate of progress. The most commonly used definition of "effect size" is an index that measures the strength of the association between one variable and another; for example, between student achievement and an intervention. These indices take different forms depending on the measure being used. The most commonly reported effect size measure is Cohen's d, which is used to compare the means of two groups. Exactly what to use to calculate d requires careful thought, because there are different options, which have different advantages and disadvantages. A more detailed explanation of the calculation and interpretation of effect sizes, along with tables to help people avoid traps and make the calculations easier, can be found in the *How Much Difference Does it Make?* brochure written by Ian Schagen and Edith Hodgen and available from either the NZCER or Ministry of Education websites (http://www.nzcer.org.nz or http://www.educationcounts.govt.nz/publications/schooling). Note that any effect size should be calculated along with a confidence interval to take into account the anticipated variability of the measures. Once calculated, effect sizes and their confidence intervals can be used to compare progress measured using different tests.

Achieving sustainable data collection and analysis

Some of the ideas and suggestions outlined in this chapter may challenge the skills of teachers and school leaders. It may be unrealistic to expect that school staff will assess students, store the data, work out the appropriate analyses to answer the questions they want answered about the impact of their practice and conduct the analyses required—with no external help. However, there are advantages for schools to be able to carry out all of this for themselves. In the standards environment schools are entering now there will certainly be a requirement for school staff to understand a number of measures and be able to interpret information based on them.

> Aim to build data expertise within the school. Seek external help when needed.

The relationship we consider most advantageous is one of interdependence with external experts (as outlined in Chapter Two). This means schools take ownership of the planning and execution of the whole data collection and recording process. They may seek input on the type of information they need to include to answer particular questions. They carry out the basic analyses that are most suitable for their immediate needs and ensure the appropriate data storage required for these and other purposes. A school may, however, need help setting up analyses to calculate effect sizes, or analyses that compare groups. So, where necessary, they should draw on external expertise to guide and help them.

The major dimensions involved in ensuring quality achievement data concern aligning the purpose with the tools or means selected to collect the data, and ensuring that:

- data are collected that allow an examination of various possible explanations for the patterns shown in the data
- data are collected and stored in a way that allows conclusions to be drawn about progress over time
- data are trustworthy
- data allow a fair and accurate assessment of performance.

In Table 7.3 a description is given of the characteristics a school might exhibit if they were operating at a basic level with respect to these dimensions. Because so many of the features are dichotomous, a middle ground was difficult to describe, so only the characteristics associated with performance at a more integrated level are given for comparison. A school that is at a mixed or middle level would likely display some but not all aspects of a statement in the higher, integrated column and may even display some aspects of a basic level.

Table 7.3 A continuum of capability: Ensuring quality student achievement data

	Basic	**Integrated**
Purpose for collecting assessment data established and tools/ processes aligned	The purpose(s) for the data are unclear and/or the tool does not align well with the purpose (e.g., the purpose is diagnostic or formative, but the assessment does not provide appropriate detail).	The main or multiple purposes are recognised; assessment means are planned to ensure each is met adequately.
Data that allow explanation (e.g., the relationship between variable and practice)	There are no or limited supplementary data collected or recorded to allow the exploration of key variables (e.g., gender, ethnicity). Recording systems are geared to annual reporting.	Research plus a theory for improvement inform the selection of explanatory variables; appropriate data are collected. Accurate identifiers for individuals allow matching of data.
Data that allow progress over time to be examined	The assessment tool does not allow judgements to be made about progress or rate (no norms, different tools at time points). Old data may be stored or archived, but they are not used.	A standardised measure with norms is included; the same measure is used over time to determine progress. A database is constructed for multiple entries per individual using accurate identifiers for individuals.

Trustworthiness of data	There are no shared processes in place to ensure any assessment takes place consistently (e.g., across students, contexts or times).	There are clearly understood shared processes, and consistency of implementation is monitored.
	Scoring consistency: moderation is ad hoc, and relies on agreement among the participants without external checking	There is shared understanding of criteria among staff, checked against external expert review, etc.
	There is little or no systematic checking of the usefulness and accuracy of what is recorded.	There is systematic checking of data to ensure they are "clean" and entered in a form that allows them to meet the purposes.
Ensuring a fair and accurate assessment of performance	There is over-reliance on a single measure to make judgements, and limited cross-checking.	Multiple sources of evidence are planned for, including *how* they will be integrated into a judgement.

Factors to consider in a standards framework

All of the previous discussion is relevant in the standards environment, but there are a number of features regarding data analysis and use that need to be highlighted in this context. First, the notion of overall teacher judgement and the use of a range of evidence means that schools need to plan carefully exactly what measures will be employed, and what type of information from what sources of evidence will be recorded systematically. Systems need to be set up accordingly. There needs to be consideration of how measures will be used to cross-check and establish the overall judgement. How will professional and internal measures be moderated, including against external criteria (such as a standardised measure)?

Progress over time is a vital ingredient in a standards framework, and the longitudinal use of data that track individual students has not been a strength of most schools. In a standards environment it will be necessary to track individuals by recording information from a range of measures in order to report progress.

Conclusion

Although we have been largely focusing on recording data from more planned assessments such as tests, the analysis of student achievement data with a view to measuring progress should be seen as complementing the assessment for learning practice of teachers. Some of the more diagnostic measures of student achievement act as planned formative assessment measures for teachers in classrooms. But teachers also collect day-to-day information about student learning to use in the classroom to inform instruction, and to move learning forward. The use of a range of sources of data—from interactive formative assessment to more planned assessment (Cowie & Bell, 1999) and formal tests—will be a feature of the standards environment. Planning the measures a school will use to gain information about student achievement relative to a standard, and how the information from the STAR stanine distribution for time 1 and time 2 from various sources will be moderated, recorded and analysed to determine student achievement and progress, are major considerations for schools. The ideas conveyed here are intended to help this process.

References

Cowie, B., & Bell, B. (1999). A model of formative assessment in science education. *Assessment in Education, 6,* 101–116.

Schagen, I., & Hodgen, E. (2009). *How much difference does it make?* Retrieved from http://www.nzcer.org.nz and www.educationcounts.govt.nz/publications/schooling

Glossary of statistical terms

Accelerated progress: greater progress than expected taking only maturation into account, or when students show greater improvement in their achievement levels within a particular length of time than we would otherwise expect.

Average: a term loosely used to indicate a typical measure. More precise terms for an average are:

> **mean:** the total of all the measures divided by the number of measures (e.g., the mean for a class test is the total of the test marks divided by the number of students writing the test)

> **median:** if all the measures are arranged in ascending (or descending) order, the median is the one right in the middle (e.g., the student with the median mark has half of the class getting a higher mark than they did, and half of the class getting a lower mark)

> **mode:** the measure that is most common (e.g., for a STAR test, the mode nationally is stanine 5, because more students achieve a stanine 5 score than any other; this would not be true in an underachieving school, where the mode might be stanine 2 or even 1, if most students in that school achieved at that level).

Bar chart: a type of graph used to show a distribution across only a few categories (e.g., gender, or ethnicity, or stanine scores). The heights of the bars show how many individuals fall into each category.

Confidence interval: when we estimate something like a mean test score for a cluster, or an effect size, it is helpful to have an indication of how accurate the estimate is likely to be. A confidence interval is defined by its upper and lower limits, and we can say with a known level of confidence (in the statistical sense) how likely it is that the true value of what we are estimating lies between these limits. For example, if an effect size of 0.30 has a 95 percent confidence interval of 0.15 to 0.45, then most probably the effect size really is within that range (it is unlikely to be either bigger or smaller).

Distribution: this refers to how measures are spread across their possible range. For example, for STAR, the possible range is stanines 1–9, and the distribution is shown by plotting a bar graph showing how many (or what percentage) of students achieve in each stanine group. Distributions are often described as being *symmetrical*, if as many students do well as do poorly (the national norms are symmetric), or *skewed*, if more students do well (or poorly) than otherwise.

Effect size: a standardised measure (free of the original units of measure, such as temperature, or asTTle score) of the difference between two groups, which takes into account the variability in the measures but not the size of the groups. It can be used to make comparisons with other measures.

Expectation: here the term is used to refer to what student progress we would expect within a particular length of time, based on the national norms for a test.

Maturation: here the term is used to refer to the expected growth in student achievement we would expect within a particular length of time if the individual continued at their current rate of progress.

Progress: here the term is used to refer to a change in the ability of students over time.

Regression to the mean: the tendency of measures, repeated over a long period, to become more average. A tall father is more likely to have sons who are shorter than him than not. A student performing exceptionally well in one test is more likely to have slightly lower marks in the next. This phenomenon becomes an issue when a group is selected *on the basis of their extreme measures* (the best/worst 20 percent, say), because that same group is almost certain to have more average measures on the next occasion due to regression to the mean. It is therefore more difficult in the case of these subgroups to tell whether any progress observed is due to an intervention, or solely regression to the mean.

Standard deviation: a measure of the typical variability in a set of data. It is a measure of how much the data points vary about their mean.

CHAPTER EIGHT

Evidence-Informed Discussions: The Role of Pedagogical Content Knowledge

Mei Lai and Stuart McNaughton

Schools are becoming increasingly focused on collecting and using evidence to improve their teaching practices and raise student achievement. By "evidence" we mean the broad range of data that are appropriate to improve teaching and learning, such as student achievement information from assessments, overall teacher judgements relating to the standards, observations of teaching practice (including observations of students) and students' beliefs from student surveys. The inquiry cycle (detailed descriptions of the inquiry cycle are provided in Chapter One) indicates that it is important to collect evidence on students to understand students' learning needs, and evidence on teachers and leaders to understand what they need to know and do to support students for the purposes of improvement.

Most schools choose to analyse and interpret their evidence collaboratively in professional learning communities, such as at department meetings, in syndicate teams or across the whole staff. The content of these discussions often becomes the basis of school-wide and classroom planning. Such "evidence-informed discussions" are therefore central to building schools' capability to analyse and use data to inform teaching.

In this chapter we briefly consider the elements that go into effective evidence-informed discussions, including interpersonal relationships, the quality of the evidence and the willingness of participants to learn from evidence. We then want to emphasise one part of what the participants bring to the conversations, which we think needs further consideration if the conversations are to be as effective as possible. This is what has been called pedagogical content knowledge (PCK): the day-to-day knowledge of how students understand and misunderstand their subjects, how to diagnose and anticipate such misunderstandings and how to deal with them when they arise (Darling-Hammond & Bransford, 2005). Such knowledge is fundamental to developing instructional capability. PCK is not about generic teaching skills, such as knowing about particular types of feedback or the role of expectations in selecting tasks. It is about the content-specific aspects of instruction, such as how the timing of the correction of a miscue in reading affects a Year 1 reader's self-corrections, or how, in Year 9, to anticipate and address the fact that students can become confused when considering the idea of audience in narratives that are very familiar, such as well-known soap operas. A mathematical example might be how to resolve the paradox for students that multiplying "lower" negative numbers (e.g., -5 compared with -2) results in "greater" values. A teacher's PCK relates to knowing about these content-specific aspects of instruction, knowing how to identify them during their lessons and/or from other evidence (e.g., assessments) and knowing how to address them. Teachers also need to know about the most useful forms of representations of ideas and concepts; the powerful analogies, illustrations, examples, explanations and demonstrations to aid student understanding. What makes the learning of specific aspects (topics) easy or difficult are the conceptions and preconceptions that students of different ages and backgrounds or cultural identities bring.

Deep knowledge of the subject domain or content is the foundation of PCK, but it is not sufficient; pedagogical knowledge is necessary, but again it is not sufficient. Both are critical. Content knowledge relates to the central concepts and practices in the domain area, such as knowledge of fractions in mathematics and solving problems using fractions. In literacy, content knowledge includes knowledge of the features of text, including structures commonly associated with different communicative intentions. This enables engagement in wide reading, with understanding across genres and writing for different purposes. Without deep knowledge of the content, it is impossible to know how students understand

and misunderstand a subject in order to anticipate problems that may arise. For example, a teacher who does not have a good grasp of fractions will have difficulty anticipating how a student might understand or misunderstand fractions and will, therefore, be less aware of how to teach the subject and monitor student understanding.

Greater PCK enhances the collegial discussion around achievement data, because practitioners are better able to pinpoint the teaching and school practices that might contribute to the achievement patterns. They are also more likely to have knowledge of a range of strategies to address the achievement patterns, which they can discuss and evaluate with other members of their professional learning community.

A brief context: Evidence-informed discussions in New Zealand

There have been positive changes in how schools analyse, use and discuss evidence to inform their teaching practices. Research on the first schooling improvement initiatives in the late 1990s showed that schools generally did not analyse and use achievement data to inform their school programmes (Robinson, Phillips, & Timperley, 2002). This finding contributed to a greater focus on doing so across schooling improvement initiatives and other national projects.

Recent research has indicated that many teachers and school leaders in New Zealand schooling improvement initiatives are regularly analysing and using evidence to refine their teaching practices, and in some studies this process was explicitly linked to improved student achievement (Lai, McNaughton, Amituanai-Toloa, Turner, & Hsiao, 2009; Timperley & Parr, 2009). However, a recent analysis of the use of assessment evidence suggests that improving PCK would help teachers to apply the information gained from their inquiry which, in turn, leads to greater improvements in achievement (Parr & Timperley, 2008).

The model for evidence-informed discussions

Earl and Timperley (2008) have proposed a model for evidence-informed conversations which consists of three dimensions: relationships of respect and challenge; how to use relevant data (i.e., the range of evidence needed); and having an inquiry habit of mind (see Figure 8.1). Since these dimensions are elaborated in Earl and Timperley (2008), we will only briefly describe each dimension here.

Figure 8.1 Processes for evidence-informed conversations

Evidence-informed Conversations

Relationships of respect
and challenge

**Evidence-informed
Conversations**

Using relevent data   Inquiry habit of mind

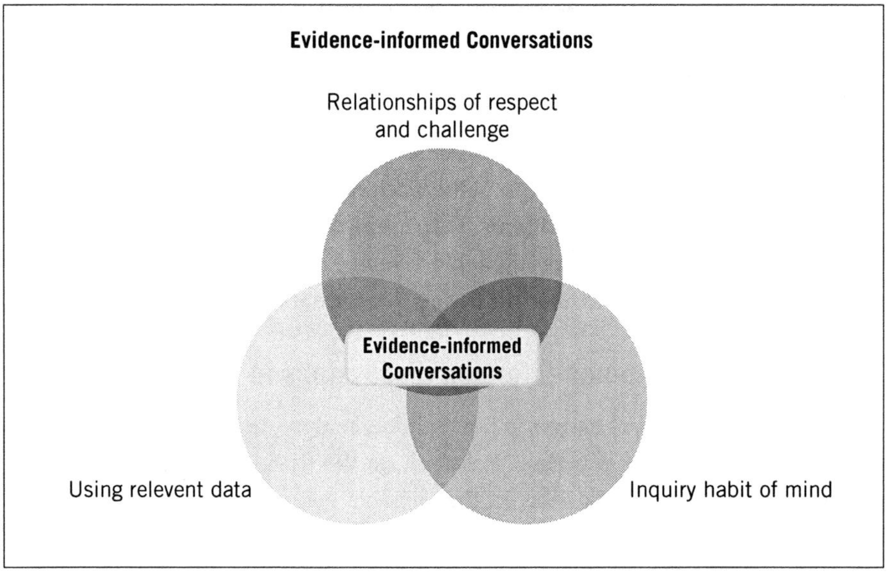

Source: Earl and Timperley (2008).

The first dimension is "relationships of respect and challenge". This means that participants in a professional learning community need to be able to challenge each other's ideas while maintaining respectful relationships. One useful framework for ensuring relationships of respect and challenge is learning conversations (Robinson & Lai, 2006). In learning conversations, participants learn how to test collectively their own and others' assumptions by clearly stating the issue/concern, treating the issue as a *fallible conclusion* not a taken-for-granted truth, testing the claims behind the conclusion and inviting others to do the same.

The second dimension in the model of evidence-informed discussions is using relevant data (Earl & Timperley, 2008). To use relevant data there needs to be a clear purpose so that participants can seek out the data that will enable them to deepen their understanding and achieve their purposes (rather than using data that are easily available but not relevant to the participants' purposes). Understanding of purposes needs to be shared and might include, for example, their contribution to making overall teacher judgements on particular standards. Participants need to recognise sound and unsound data; that is, they need to be able to judge the quality of the data so that decisions are not based on inaccurate or misleading evidence. This requires, in turn, some understanding of measurement (including the statistical concepts identified in Chapter Seven), because important information on student learning comes from assessments. Finally, it is important to ensure valid interpretations of the data.

The third dimension in the model is having an inquiry habit of mind. It is all too easy to fall into "activity traps": moving quickly to doing, to being busy and to feeling productive without sufficient attention paid to selecting the right things to do in the circumstances (Katz, Earl, & Ben Jaafar, in press). Linking inquiry to a habit of mind emphasises the fact that inquiry is *a way of thinking* that involves an ongoing process of using data to make decisions. This process involves a series of discussions that move towards clearer directions and decisions, and that draw on, or seek out, information as participants become closer to understanding the problem they are trying to solve. The process also requires participants to:

- value deep understanding rather than "quick-fix" solutions, based on inadequate understanding of the problem that is tackled
- reserve judgement
- have tolerance for ambiguity
- take a range of perspectives
- pose increasingly focused questions.

PCK and data discussions

There is a key component in the model that we want to consider in greater depth. It is the PCK required for teachers to be able to identify precisely students' learning needs from achievement information and analyses of teaching in order to develop teaching practices based on needs. PCK is therefore an integral part of the model dimension "Using relevant data". Our emphasis here is on teachers' capacity to do so collectively through professional learning communities rather than individually.

If teachers are to use their PCK to develop more effective teaching practices based on evidence (student achievement data, analyses of teaching practices), then the quality of evidence needs to be sound and the type of evidence discussed appropriate. For teachers, this includes good diagnostic information from valid assessments for every student in their class to allow them to identify how each student performs in relation to expectations, such as the newly developed standards, and to identify through more or less formal activities the learning needs of each student. Both types of information are needed to plan a teaching programme to meet students' needs. The most useful assessments for teachers are, therefore, those that reveal students' strengths and learning needs relative to an agreed reference point. Typical reference points are nationally determined norms, the standards themselves and national curriculum levels.

It is important to analyse data to identify if there are any subgroups of students that teachers might focus on in their class. For example, the data might indicate that half the class has no idea of structure in text aiming to persuade, or that male students struggle with the surface features of writing more than the deeper features. Some indication of how other students in the school are performing helps the teacher interpret his/her results in the context of the school (e.g., perhaps the whole school needs support in meeting the standard, not just his/her class), and could identify areas of common need across classrooms that can be addressed by a school-wide programme. Teachers also need diagnostic information about their own teaching practices through feedback from other teachers, senior managers or external facilitators, or through their own self-reflection based on evidence.

For senior managers, having high-quality appropriate evidence might mean aggregated evidence for each classroom and subgroup (e.g., by year level, ethnicity) in their school. Evidence needs to include performance against the national standards, and needs to identify commonalities in student learning needs across classrooms, as well as providing information about teachers' and leaders' (including their own) learning needs, to help the senior managers determine how best to support teachers and leaders to support their students. This process becomes a cycle of inquiry for school leaders.

Why is PCK important when discussing evidence?

The goal of many evidence-informed discussions is to improve school and teaching practices to enhance student learning outcomes. The purpose is therefore not just to "read" a graph or table of the data (e.g., "there are 10 students not reading at the standard"; "almost all students did not understand the learning intention"), but also to work out what students need to learn to do next, and how to teach students effectively to learn those aspects they are weak at.

If teachers do not have sufficient PCK to know what to do next, then they can become frustrated at having identified a problem for which they don't know the solution. One teacher participating in the Building Evaluative Capability in Schooling Improvement Project noted in a feedback meeting that if you don't know how to improve your teaching, then inquiring 10 more times is not going to help you come up with a more effective teaching practice. Sometimes you just need to be told what practices you might be able to use.

Without extensive PCK, teachers may also nominate a range of strategies that may or may not be effective, and other teachers in the professional learning community (who, similarly, may not have sufficient PCK) might not be able to evaluate whether the strategies proposed are more or less effective to address the student learning needs that have been identified. This may result in the teachers applying strategies that are inappropriate to solve the problem or, worse, are detrimental to student learning.

What does PCK look like in the context of evidence-informed discussions?

We described PCK at the beginning of this paper: PCK is the knowledge of how students understand and misunderstand their subjects, how teachers diagnose and anticipate misunderstandings, and how to deal with misunderstandings when they arise. We also noted that it is dependent on deep domain or content knowledge. In the context of evidence-informed discussions, PCK refers to teachers' knowledge of individual-, classroom- and school-level evidence about students' learning and knowledge of specific literacy practices associated with effective learning (Parr & Timperley, 2008). This requires teachers to be highly specific (not generic) about students' needs, and to select or access knowledge about teaching that is appropriate to identified needs.

We briefly report here on two evidence-informed discussions that illustrate the PCK required for effective discussions. In other chapters in this book the continuum from basic, middle/mixed to integrated has largely been presented in the form of sets of descriptors. In this chapter we have illustrated the continuum through transcripts of conversations.

The first set of conversations, illustrating a middle/mixed point on the continuum, are from two decile 1 schools that were making progress greater than nationally expected in reading comprehension, and had achievement levels close to national averages. In these conversations, the discussions were specifically contextualised to the student learning needs identified in the data, in that the group discussed the learning needs from the achievement data before discussing the strategies to solve them.

The first transcript is from a school in which a small syndicate team is discussing how to improve achievement over the summer holidays. The school had previously examined their achievement data and identified the drop in achievement over summer as a particularly pressing problem for the school. The possible PCK which contributes to the discussion is commented on here (although to determine the exact nature of the PCK would require probes and debriefing). PCK is described as conditional here because it is only part of the knowledge needed. It largely involves identifying the nature of the particular problems being discussed, because knowing about the problem is a precondition for thinking about what the constraints and solutions might be.

The following are excerpts from real conversations, which we have reported in full here. They took place in very specific contexts, including a history of evidence-based conversations at the school and cluster levels. They probably represent a middle/mixed level in terms of the level of the discussion, as the knowledge seems to represent knowledge about pedagogy rather than knowledge of content from the point of view of teaching it to others. With hindsight, and with the luxury of time to evaluate the conversations, we can see how the conversations might be enhanced, and we talk about this later.

Transcript	Example of conditional PCK
Team leader: We continually talk about this every year at conferences—there are the kids who fall through after the holidays. It's not just 15 [students], all of our Year 7s. It's right across the board. How do we make constructive the learning over the holidays to ensure that the kids gain mileage, maximise mileage, out of what they do in the holidays and not just simply saying read, "Read more"?	Knowledge that there are substantial practice effects related to reading comprehension, and that the drops in summer are related to this. Students, even at Years 4–6, need structure, either in terms of the preparation from school or the activities/practices at home, in order to capitalise on the learning experiences over summer.

Teacher 1: Maybe we should perhaps have a trip to the library. *Teacher 2:* At the beginning of the year or before? *Team leader:* At the end of the year. *Teacher 1:* Perhaps even before the end of the year. It's only up the road … Invite the parents to come along as well. Maybe parents don't realise it's free to join. *Team leader:* The holiday programme? *Teacher 1:* Yes they have lots of holiday programmes, and they are not confined to the one here. Once parents join they can go anywhere in Manukau. There are libraries that are open Saturdays as well.	Knowledge that the library can be used as a resource, but that the resource needs to be "primed" by teachers and others so that students develop familiarity with the resource and patterns of use. Knowledge of the role of parents in using the library as a resource.
Team leader: I've also got some stuff from *Newspapers in Education*. I will actually email [librarian] and find out if they have holiday programmes coming up, features that we could alert parents to while they are on holiday. The Treaty of Waitangi is coming up when we come back [to school], and then there's only a week before the Treaty and we do a massive burst within a week. Really it should start over the holidays, possibly tracking down with *The Herald* the Treaty of Waitangi. OK, talk to the kids about these—the articles coming in *The Herald* … It's walking distance to the library and we get the parents to come down.	Knowledge that learning and teaching can be very effectively driven by well-chosen topics. Choosing a powerful topic provides a knowledge base and focus for teaching and learning, but actively selecting topic studies depends on resources (availability, relevance and topicality).
Teacher: Yes, absolutely. You need to get them on board because the children cannot do it alone. You need that partnership between the school and home.	Knowing that parents being involved in their child's school learning can add considerable value to their learning at school. Implied in this is that a partnership is required, and depending on what is known about "partnerships" this might have further implications for teachers and their teaching.

The second transcript is from a staff meeting where the staff have been discussing the achievement trends using STAR in their school, in particular the high scores in Subtests 1 and 2 (Decoding and Sentence Comprehension) and the lower scores in Subtests 3 and 4 (Paragraph Comprehension and Vocabulary).

Transcript	Example of conditional PCK
Teacher 1: We need to go back to that accelerated learning, don't we? We know from looking at those previous graphs we have still got some kids who are maintaining or making expected gains but not accelerating … So that brings us to the interpretation. What might be causing these results? And some of this really ties up to our strengths and weaknesses. Yes, we could say grammar, I think, is what is causing the results, and children not being grammatical they write what they speak. Teachers will become more explicit, and explicit acts of teaching are basically what are needed. That explicit teaching is also reinforced as part of homework. I noticed when we look through homework books that there are passages that you have stuck purposely in there for their homework to do, so that they are also doing it at home. What else could be causing those results if we go back to the results? *Teacher 2:* Specific teaching strategies … Yes, we are doing more activities; comprehension, you know, to back up and focus on. We are more aware of it, I guess, we are more aware of what our kids need.	Knowledge that teaching and learning rates need to be accelerated and that there are specific areas needing explicit instruction. The content knowledge relating to reading comprehension is built up from repeated and extensive engagement with texts so that students, like their teachers, come to recognise and understand the ways the texts work, including the role of grammar. In this sense, homework can potentially add to the extensive practice, providing an additional opportunity to influence rates of learning.

Teacher 1:	Knowing that developing student monitoring
I think some of the reasons why the results are showing what they are showing are because there are discussions with the children about what they have scored, and that's through their learning journals. If you go and look at their portfolios, they have got a sheet there that says in Term 1 you scored stanine 4 and then it shows whether they've made progress, and so the kids know exactly in Term 1 their learning journal goes home with that portfolio, oh I've got a stanine 4 so maybe the next time I do it I can get a stanine 5 or 6. So they have got something to work towards. I think that is part of it as well.	of their own progress and developing resources such as a portfolio (and providing guidance for that monitoring) are powerful ways of involving students in their own learning. Producing good readers (and hence the development of effective reading comprehension) depends on developing awareness of what and how one reads for different purposes and meanings. The knowledge is about the importance of making learning from extensive reading visible for students.
Teacher 3: What about the test being a mystery? I know it is something that is done and talked about. You know, they don't just do it and it disappears off somewhere else: it is done and we talk about it and we talk about what we've done well, what wasn't done well, and they have their input too.	
Teacher 4: So you are using the data with the kids as well.	
Teacher 3: It's no secret.	

One important way these conversations might be enhanced so that they exemplify a more integrated level of conversation relates to precision in the use of concepts and how articulated and generalised the knowledge is. In the second transcript, for example, the conversation could have been enhanced by the teacher being more specific about the kinds of explicit strategies that were required to address the issues identified in the data. However, to be fair, in a single transcript one concept may be referred to that encompasses detailed knowledge that has been shared previously, and we don't know how these conversations have developed over time.

We don't wish to suggest that at every meeting explicit comments and systematic elaboration of all PCK-informed ideas should take place. This could lead to very boring meetings that exhaust teachers and don't motivate anyone to change their practices. There may be a developmental progression in how teachers come to have greater precision in their conversations in which some statements are shorthand for a great deal of shared knowledge. Nevertheless, to illustrate how we should think about PCK, what follows is a short, idealised example made up from segments of conversations at several schools. We have compiled this to illustrate what discussion at an integrated level *might* look like.

Idealised transcript	Example of PCK
Team leader: So, summarising, we need to get the rate of learning vocabulary up. We need to figure out several things: where we have the greatest impact and what we should target. *Teacher 3:* The biggest problem for our kids is not all the words but just some of the words in their books. They can get the topic words, and they get a lot of the technical words we use for intentions and strategies, but the ones that throw them are the unusual ones or the metaphors, or the ones that have a new meaning. *Teacher 1:* Yes I remember we were reading in my class a book on Alexander the Great and I came to the sentence "The army was divided upon itself". They didn't get that. I reminded them of the meaning in our maths work and then said what it meant. They got the idea. Layla said it was like the All Blacks on a bad day!	Knowledge that a focus on vocabulary involves increasing the rate of learning words (implied here is that learning needs to be accelerated compared to usual rates to enable students to get to the levels needed). Also, knowledge of the domain suggests that the more words one knows and the more connections between those words (e.g., semantically and morphologically) that are made, the faster the rate of acquiring new words that are related. In this situation, teachers show knowledge that two specific focuses are needed: on some types of words (e.g., known words that are used in unusual ways, such as the metaphorical, and figurative uses, primarily associated with written language), and on the use of some types of approaches (and these will need special attention). The teacher recalls a specific instance of the general point, which exemplifies the PCK about words and how types of words (and uses in sentences) can be problematic for these particular children. The teacher is aware of potential solutions that are evidence-based in practice.

Team leader: That is a good point to start talking about how we do this. What works best?	
Teacher 2: Well, that example of shared reading is a good one and I have found that if I elaborate words and phrases and sentences, then that builds meaning. But you know what? It means I have to read the book first and target likely words. If I don't, I have to scramble to think. Even the dictionary might not help. I don't always get it right, and then I model searching for the meanings.	The PCK here is specific evidence that an approach works well but also what some of the constraints on this might be: in this instance, the instructional implications of being prepared and also providing models for how to solve the problem.
Teacher 3: Yes I have found too that I have to repeat the words or the phrases. We go around using them in class and the children get excited and really quite proud of themselves. Huata went around saying "desist from grabbing my book" for days. But that's good, the motivation was there and that's how we learn isn't it?	The shared PCK is developed further by referring to the need for extended and elaborated practice. Also acknowledged is the need for motivating the children to learn further—technically called (in the literature) "word consciousness".
Teacher 4: I make sure in our cameo writing I point out how words are used. I need to teach them that it is OK to try these out and even play with the words in their writing—when it's appropriate.	The discussion about approaches continues to develop PCK, this time about possibilities in writing. The knowledge includes the need to explicitly prompt children to use words and sentences. This is an issue to do with meta-linguistic awareness as well as learning intentions (including that it is OK to use others' writing).
Team leader: There is quite a lot of research evidence for what you are saying. The approaches we can use include shared reading, reading to kids and writing approaches like cameo writing, as you say. But the preparation and careful attention to the words and their complex meanings is important. And like learning a new language, practice across oral and written language is essential. It's like building a community of "word detectives". They also need strategies so that [they] are not dependent on us to always point it out—that word consciousness that we read about in the resource is important.	The team leader makes connections with the research literature. The personalised knowledge in the teachers' PCK needs to be connected with information in resources that have been available and that are part of the shared formal knowledge. Importantly, the PCK the team leader has enables teachers to connect technical concepts with actual instructional practices.

Our experience working with clusters of schools suggests that teachers initially need to learn to extract the relevant information from evidence of achievement. Once they can identify general trends over time, they learn how to identify specific issues in the data, which they can address in their classrooms. An important feature of professional learning communities is that the knowledge required for effective evidence-informed discussions can be shared, thus building instructional capability. This means that anyone's knowledge can be augmented and complemented by the particular areas of strength other teachers might have. The professional learning community as a whole acts to solve problems that support the practices teachers have in their own classrooms.

However, if teachers have limited content knowledge and few strategies to move learning forward by solving the problems identified in the data, they may need to be taught a range of possible strategies, including how to select appropriate strategies (this would include a more conceptual understanding of the rationale for the strategy) and how to apply them to the problems identified in the data. Literacy leaders in the school and/or senior managers (e.g., principals, deputy principals) may have sufficient pedagogical content knowledge to develop this in their teachers through in-school professional learning experiences and the use of relevant supporting resources (e.g., the Assessment Resource Banks). However, solving more complex or challenging problems might require interdependence with knowledgeable experts such as other school leaders and teachers, researchers and/or professional developers.

We conclude this chapter by presenting a continuum of capability for evaluating the level of PCK required for effective evidence-informed discussions (Table 8.1). This continuum will support teachers and school leaders to identify their current levels of capability and understand what they might need to do to further develop their capability.

Table 8.1 A continuum of capability: Evaluating PCK for effective evidence-informed discussions

	Basic	Mixed (equivalent to "conditional")	Integrated
Knowledge of subject content	Teacher knowledge of the domain/content is assumed, not tested. Little effort is made to ascertain and specify the content knowledge required in areas of student need. There is no *collective* reflection on their own or others' knowledge.	There is no assumption that all teachers possess knowledge of the domain/content, but this is inquired into largely through self-report. There are attempts to specify the aspects of content knowledge required in the area of student need. There is some collective reflection on own and others' knowledge, but this is inquired into largely through self-report and/or based on anecdotal evidence.	There is systematic inquiry into relevant teacher content knowledge. Careful delineation of content knowledge is needed to address student learning needs. Critical reflection on own and others' knowledge is linked with theory, research and professional evidence.
Knowledge of teaching it to others	The nature (cause and developmental course) of the student difficulty/misunderstanding is described in general terms. The teacher is able to identify, at a general level, the practices that relate to learning need. Research-informed findings regarding practices relating to learning need are not articulated. There is no *collective* reflection on own or others' knowledge.	The teacher is able to diagnosis specifically the nature of student learning need. Practice-related solutions are either not completely aligned with need (a precise link between the problem and the proposed solution is not established) and/or there is a lack of evidence of effectiveness (e.g., research). There is some collective reflection on own and others' knowledge, but inquired into largely through self-report and/or based on anecdotal evidence.	There is a detailed understanding of the nature of student learning need, in context. Specific, high-leverage, evidence-based solutions applicable to both the learning need and the current context are articulated (and the rationale is supplied). The means of checking the efficacy of each practice solution are clear. There is critical reflection on own and others' knowledge, based on evidence of an understanding of the student need in context.

Reflection questions

QUESTION

In the light of the transcripts presented above, consider the last meeting where patterns of student achievement were discussed.

Were teachers and/or school leaders able to diagnose specific students' learning needs from the achievement information, or did they describe generic strategies (e.g., improve reading comprehension), which may not be applicable to the specific students' learning needs?

a Do you think that teachers and/or school leaders have sufficient PCK to diagnose specific students' learning needs, and develop ways of addressing those needs?

b If not, what support in developing PCK should be provided to teachers/school leaders?

References

Darling-Hammond, L., & Bransford, J. (2005). *Preparing teachers for a changing world: What teachers should be able to learn and be able to do.* San Francisco: John Wiley & Sons.

Earl, L., & Timperley, H. (Eds.). (2008). *Evidence-based conversations to improve educational practices.* Dordrecht, Netherlands: Kluwer/Springer Academic Publishers.

Katz, S., Earl, L., & Ben Jaafar, S. (forthcoming). *Networking schools for learning.* Thousand Oaks, CA: Corwin Press.

Lai, M. K., McNaughton, S., Amituanai-Toloa, M., Turner, R., & Hsiao, S. (2009). Sustained acceleration of achievement in reading comprehension: The New Zealand experience. *Reading Research Quarterly, 44*(1), 30–56.

Parr, J., & Timperley, H. (2008). Teachers, schools and using evidence: Consideration of preparedness. *Assessment in Education: Principles, Policy and Practice, 15*(1), 57–71.

Robinson, V. M. J., & Lai, M. K. (2006). *Practitioner research for educators: A guide to improving classrooms and schools.* Thousand Oaks, CA: Corwin Press.

Robinson, V. M. J., Phillips, G., & Timperley, H. (2002). Using achievement data for school-based curriculum review: A bridge too far? *Leadership and Policy in Schools, 1*(1), 3–29.

Timperley, H., & Parr, J. (2009). Chain of influence from policy to practice in the New Zealand literacy strategy. *Research Papers in Education: Policy and Practice, 24*(2), 135–154.

CHAPTER NINE

Where to From Here? Taking Stock and Engaging in Meta-Inquiry

Judy Parr and Helen Timperley

In this book our central theme has been inquiry for the improvement of schools: inquiry that involves evidence, particularly evidence of student achievement, including achievement in relation to standards. Our aim in this concluding chapter is twofold. First, we hope that it will prompt you to apply what you have learnt about the inquiry process to examine in depth your own school context. Second, in doing this we would like to prompt meta-inquiry; that is, for you to gain a sense of how capable you are at engaging in inquiry through examining and reflecting on your ability to conduct this process and learn from it.

The course of improvement is not one dimensional. There are multiple dimensions to attend to. Inquiry for improvement requires building capability on a number of fronts. We have talked of instructional, organisational and evaluative capability. Each chapter has endeavoured to examine aspects of these three fronts while addressing the overarching question, "What is needed to develop inquiry for building better schools?" Each chapter contains a number of messages, some of which may have a familiar ring, but other points may have been new or presented a different way of looking at things. What each of us takes from the chapters is likely to depend on our own experience and current context. We may have heard the term *theory for improvement* but not really appreciated its role and significance in striving to improve student achievement.

For those of us with Māori-medium classes in the school, the Māori-medium education chapter is likely to have prompted reflection, perhaps regarding assumptions about valued outcomes, perhaps with respect to an expectation that Māori-medium teachers will be able to accomplish the "transfer" of English-medium professional development to their setting without additional support in the form of time and expertise.

While we may be familiar with the notion of change and its attendant stressors, we may not have thought about ensuring explicit talk about change as a way of managing change.

Later chapters emphasise the centrality of knowledge—knowledge about content and pedagogical content knowledge—to effective inquiry at classroom level and within the professional learning community of the school. That should prompt us to think not only about building knowledge but also what evidence we have to assist inquiry about knowledge levels.

While appreciating the fact that there are multiple dimensions involved in improvement, it is also important to remind ourselves that the course of improvement is not necessarily linear. It may falter as we attend to a major area of need, or it may accelerate as learning enables a powerful lever to come into play (more on this later). There is a delicate balancing act required when there are multiple capabilities to build. The trick is to avoid trying to do everything at once, which may result in a sense of change chaos. Staff may feel overwhelmed and unable to see how everything fits together. Yet we need to bring about change at a pace that ensures students progress sufficiently to allow those who need to the opportunity to catch up with their peers.

The first, and possibly the primary, litmus test of evaluative capability as a school would seem to be to "take stock". (As this is done, you can reflect on your capabilities to do it.) A powerful way to take stock as a learning community might be to use the continua that have been presented and discussed in each chapter throughout the book and work through each dimension, discussing the relevant evidence that will help you to place your school in the category that provides the best fit in terms of describing your current state. This discussion is likely to surface and, hopefully, help resolve issues.

The discussion could happen in a number of forums and formats. As you will see in the three cases presented below, schools take different approaches to using the continua. The larger primary school worked in groups to complete this stocktake, presenting their conclusions with evidence to the wider staff for comment, while the smaller primary school operated as a whole staff. Leaders in the secondary school worked with a department. The smaller school felt sufficiently familiar and comfortable with the ideas contained in the inquiry cycles to hop around, switching between chapters, but the other school took a more step-by-step approach, working through methodically.

If you use a template like the one provided below (and a highlighter or similar) and shade the categories where you place your school, it will allow you at a glance to view the pattern and see the relative strengths and gaps that you, as a school, exhibit. In which chapters are there mostly "basics"? Are there other areas at the more "integrated" end? The dimensions from each chapter are included as headers for each continuum. Because they are so brief you may need to consult and reread parts of the chapter as you work through. Note that the dimensions described as part of the continua from Chapter Two give an overall sense of the part of the inquiry cycle that may need strengthening.

Following the presentation of the template, the different profiles of two primary and one secondary school are presented as case studies. The case studies describe how these schools used the template to identify the areas on which they needed to focus, and the reasons for the decisions and the actions that might be taken, given the pattern recorded.

A TEMPLATE FOR TAKING STOCK

Chapter Two (evidence and inquiry)

1. Identifying valued outcomes and student learning needs

BASIC	MIDDLE/MIXED	INTEGRATED

2. Identifying professional learning needs—leaders and teachers

BASIC	MIDDLE/MIXED	INTEGRATED

3. Engagement in professional learning to deepen knowledge and refine skills

BASIC	MIDDLE/MIXED	INTEGRATED

4. Engagement of students in new learning experiences

BASIC	MIDDLE/MIXED	INTEGRATED

Chapter Three (theory for improvement)

1. Understanding of the likely interrelated causes of the problem

BASIC	MIDDLE/MIXED	INTEGRATED

2. Proposed evidence-based solutions to directly address the causes of the problem

BASIC	MIDDLE/MIXED	INTEGRATED

3. Interim and long-term targets against which progress can be judged

BASIC	MIDDLE/MIXED	INTEGRATED

5. Ways to monitor progress towards the targets

BASIC	MIDDLE/MIXED	INTEGRATED

Chapter Four (talking about change knowledge)

1. Identifying priorities

BASIC	MIDDLE/MIXED	INTEGRATED

2. Holding high expectations

BASIC	MIDDLE/MIXED	INTEGRATED

4. Communicating challenges

BASIC	MIDDLE/MIXED	INTEGRATED

6. Evaluating outcomes

BASIC	MIDDLE/MIXED	INTEGRATED

Chapter Five (Māori-medium education)

1. Identifying valued outcomes

BASIC	MIDDLE/MIXED	INTEGRATED

2. Leadership

BASIC	MIDDLE/MIXED	INTEGRATED

3. Professional development

BASIC	MIDDLE/MIXED	INTEGRATED

4. School development

BASIC	MIDDLE/MIXED	INTEGRATED

Chapter Six (classroom practice)

1. Selecting appropriate diagnostic measures to ascertain the pattern of development

BASIC	MIDDLE/MIXED	INTEGRATED

2. Students' understanding of their goals and learning

BASIC	MIDDLE/MIXED	INTEGRATED

3. Student engagement in self-assessment

BASIC	MIDDLE/MIXED	INTEGRATED

4. Use of information about student learning to evaluate practice

BASIC	MIDDLE/MIXED	INTEGRATED

Chapter Seven (ensuring quality data)

1. The purpose of collecting data and alignment with tools

BASIC	MIDDLE/MIXED	INTEGRATED

2. Rich data to allow explanation

BASIC	MIDDLE/MIXED	INTEGRATED

3. Trustworthiness

BASIC	MIDDLE/MIXED	INTEGRATED

4. Ensuring a fair and accurate assessment

BASIC	MIDDLE/MIXED	INTEGRATED

Chapter Eight (PCK and evidence-informed discussions)

1. Knowledge of subject content

BASIC	MIDDLE/MIXED	INTEGRATED

2. Knowledge of teaching the subject to others

BASIC	MIDDLE/MIXED	INTEGRATED

When the template is completed, consider the pattern of your relative areas of strength and where it seems that work is needed. What are the key areas to work on? In addressing this question, consider what, in your context, are likely to be key levers. Key levers are aspects that, if strengthened, are likely to have a powerful impact beyond the area in which the lever is operating. The notion of key levers is an important one. Some capabilities may be more central or foundational and are needed before other aspects can develop. You might need to ensure that something is securely in place before turning to the next issue. If you don't have quality student achievement data that allow you to answer the questions you want answered, to help make informed decisions about your relative progress and impact, then, clearly, ensuring the availability of such data is paramount to effective inquiry.

Often changes in classroom practice are the key lever to improving student outcomes. Such changes then become the focus of professional development. To act as a key lever, however, data about changes in classrooms need to be linked to patterns of achievement. If, for example, after three years' working on improving student writing there seems to be no discernible progress, then the classroom data might help to provide the information needed to diagnose what is really needed to improve practice to raise writing achievement.

There are some other issues to think about in deciding what to focus on. These include the notion that some aspects may be able to be worked on in parallel without engendering a sense of being overwhelmed by the enormity of the task. Then there is the consideration that while some things may seem simple to implement, they are more difficult in practice. One example is taking action with respect to the finding that leaders who attend professional learning with their teachers so they can build their instructional capability have an impact on student achievement

(Robinson, Hōhepa, & Lloyd, 2009). It seems a relatively simple matter to decide that the principal and other senior managers will begin to attend professional development sessions to learn alongside the teachers. This apparently simple-to-implement strategy may, however, raise other issues. Learning alongside teachers might also involve leaders in examining their beliefs about their own role, so that they will need to address the reasons for their previous intermittent attendance and the implications of this for leading improvement. Not least, it involves working out how all the other things that took them away from participating with their teachers actually get done.

Three case studies with different profiles

In this section we have provided descriptions of two primary schools and one secondary school, all with differing profiles of likely capability for engaging in inquiry for improvement purposes. The descriptions are provided to illustrate the kinds of approaches you might want to use when reading this book. So as you read the cases, consider the decisions they made in the light of your own profile and context.

CASE STUDY 1: SCHOOL A

This school is a smallish primary school in a rural town. There is a principal and four staff. They have a close-knit community and the school has worked hard to include parents and wider whānau in the school. They have engaged in a particular programme that was designed to help with this. Although they have a sizeable number of Māori students, they have no Māori-medium education classes.

When this school engaged with the template, placing themselves on the continua, they discussed the evidence and made judgements as a whole staff together. They obtained reasonable consensus, sometimes after a lot of discussion and debate. At times they agreed to disagree and recorded a "half and half" or a "moving towards" type decision. It took most of their teacher-only day to take stock, but they thought it worthwhile. They had all familiarised themselves with the various continua and did not work religiously through them from Chapters Two to Eight. Instead, as they considered the dimensions of the general inquiry cycle contained in Chapter Two, they moved to chapters that examined parts of it in more detail. They may have missed the odd dimension, but this did not seem to matter in the long run because the exercise served a valuable purpose: they tested their collective evaluative capability and discovered areas to work on to ensure ongoing improvement. While the overview of their engagement with evidence and inquiry obtained from the dimensions in Chapter Two (see highlighted areas below) suggested a school pretty well equipped to use evidence as the basis for inquiry for improvement, the more detailed lens offered through the other chapters brought to light several areas that they needed to work on.

SCHOOL A's PATTERN OF DECISIONS

Chapter Two (evidence and inquiry)

1. Identifying valued outcomes and student learning needs

BASIC	MIDDLE/MIXED	INTEGRATED

2. Identifying professional learning needs—leaders and teachers

BASIC	MIDDLE/MIXED	INTEGRATED

4. Engagement in professional learning to deepen knowledge and refine skills

BASIC	MIDDLE/MIXED	INTEGRATED

5. Engagement of students in new learning experiences

BASIC	MIDDLE/MIXED	INTEGRATED

Chapter Three (theory for improvement)

1. Understanding of likely interrelated causes of the problem

BASIC	MIDDLE/MIXED	INTEGRATED

2. Proposed evidence-based solutions to directly address the causes of the problem

BASIC	MIDDLE/MIXED	INTEGRATED

3. Interim and long-term targets against which progress can be judged

BASIC	MIDDLE/MIXED	INTEGRATED

4. Ways to monitor progress towards the targets

BASIC	MIDDLE/MIXED	INTEGRATED

Chapter Four (talking about change knowledge)

1. Identifying priorities

BASIC	MIDDLE/MIXED	INTEGRATED

2. Holding high expectations

BASIC	MIDDLE/MIXED	INTEGRATED

3. Communicating challenges

BASIC	MIDDLE/MIXED	INTEGRATED

4. Evaluating outcomes

BASIC	MIDDLE/MIXED	INTEGRATED

Chapter Six (classroom practice)

1. Selecting appropriate diagnostic measures to ascertain the pattern of development

BASIC	MIDDLE/MIXED	INTEGRATED

2. Students' understanding of their goals and learning

BASIC	MIDDLE/MIXED	INTEGRATED

3. Student engagement in self-assessment

BASIC	MIDDLE/MIXED	INTEGRATED

4. Use of information about student learning to evaluate practice

BASIC	MIDDLE/MIXED	INTEGRATED

Chapter Seven (ensuring quality data)

1. The purpose of collecting and alignment with tools

BASIC	MIDDLE/MIXED	INTEGRATED

2. Rich data to allow explanation

BASIC	MIDDLE/MIXED	INTEGRATED

3. Trustworthiness

BASIC	MIDDLE/MIXED	INTEGRATED

4. Ensuring a fair and accurate assessment

BASIC	MIDDLE/MIXED	INTEGRATED

Chapter Eight (PCK and evidence-informed discussions)

1. Knowledge of subject content

BASIC	MIDDLE/MIXED	INTEGRATED

2. Knowledge of teaching the subject to others

BASIC	MIDDLE/MIXED	INTEGRATED

In terms of identifying valued outcomes and student learning needs, they agreed they had stated goals and that the means they used to record and examine student achievement data were sound. They had been part of a cluster of schools that had reached a high standard in this respect and, as a school they had learnt a great deal about collecting, storing and analysing data and using these data to formulate targets. They had several years' worth of sound data and written analyses accompanying them. The decision to place themselves at an integrated level in relation to valued outcomes and student learning needs was uncontested and straightforward.

They then switched to the dimensions from Chapter Seven concerning ensuring quality data and decided that the purpose for collecting data was clear and the tools they used were aligned with the purpose (dimension 1). Moreover, their learning from working with other schools had made them sensitive to ensuring the data were collected and recorded in a way that made them trustworthy (dimension 3). They were not so sure they had sufficiently rich data concerning things that might help explain the patterns of achievement their students were exhibiting. They certainly had data from a reading, a vocabulary and a writing assessment, and the first two at least allowed them to track individual students. (They had set up a separate database for this purpose.) But, they realised, they had no details such as attendance to link to individual students and, perhaps more significantly, no systematic information about teacher practice that could be considered in relation to the achievement data.

They decided that they needed to move next to the dimensions accompanying the classroom practice chapter (Chapter Six). But, before they did, they talked long and hard about how they came to judgements about student achievement. They were very aware of the notion of overall teacher judgement that was an integral part of decision making with respect to the national standards. Classroom teachers illustrated the wealth of assessment information they had: literacy assessment information from running records, from progression through book levels and from draft books; and the numeracy assessments from mini tests, work books and semistructured interviews. These teacher assessments were not necessarily recorded centrally, nor were they implemented in all classrooms or in the same way across classrooms. Some junior teachers, for example, recorded what they discovered students could do in writing from their conferencing and reading of drafts and final pieces. Others stored the information as mental notes. The staff all felt they had not reached the integrated level because they could not claim to have an "audit trail" to record the pieces of information used to make overall judgements about the level of performance of the students.

They now turned their attention to the dimensions from the classroom practice chapter because the classroom had moved centre stage when they talked of rich data to allow explanation, and then when they thought about a fair and accurate assessment through using a range of assessment means and cross-checking, etc. Dimension 1, about diagnostic measures, prompted some debate over whether the information obtained from the standardised measure they were using was really useful for planning instruction but, in the final analysis, they decided it was adequate when supplemented by information from other sources.

The students' understanding of what and why they were learning particular things was deemed to be at a high level. This was something that had been developed as part of the programme aimed at enhancing the involvement of parents and whānau. Students were able to take school work home and explain to their family what it was they were learning and the reason for it, and even about their pattern of strength and needs with respect to aspects of various areas of the curriculum. But, the teachers realised, this did not mean that students could engage in self-assessment; that is, work out for themselves where they were in terms of performance and what they needed to be focusing on to reach the desired level. This was an area they felt was underdeveloped. While the idea of students explaining to parents about their learning was designed to enable parents to be more of a resource, the teachers felt that with the concept of self-assessment they were missing a potential powerful resource for learning. They resolved to check out what students could do in this regard and they earmarked this as something for their professional learning communities to discuss so that they could begin the process of scaffolding their students into the area of self-assessment.

The fourth dimension within classroom practice—use of information about student learning to evaluate practice—was an interesting one. The teachers in this school had well-functioning professional learning communities. They were accustomed to deprivatised practice. They had a sufficient sense of trust that they shared videos of their practice with colleagues in their professional learning communities and engaged in critique of practice. They had high expectations of one another as professionals who were engaged in ongoing learning; they appreciated that knowledge was not static, and that even in their fairly stable community students were not experiencing the same out-of-school context as five years ago. They did admit, though, that the critique was pretty much critique of one's own practice rather than the practice of others.

This observation caused them to veer off momentarily to the dimension in the professional learning chapter regarding challenging talk, and the consensus was that they could up the ante in this regard. But the big learning for them was that for all of their discussion and deconstruction of practice, they actually did not link the details or elements of an individual teacher's practice to details of the pattern in student learning—the pattern of strengths and gaps. Some wanted to place their level at basic; others felt it was more mixed. Both camps felt this was a crucial aspect of instructional and evaluative capability which they needed to strengthen. They resolved to draft a description of practices and assemble an observational tool to help them view practice more systematically, but this faltered when they could not get agreement on what it was they were going to home in on with respect to practice. As one teacher observed, you cannot look at everything: you have to focus on what matters. But what practices matter?

The talk about what particular practices were likely to address what particular needs led one teacher (or was it the principal?) to challenge them to state their "theory for improvement". This, she said, would help them clarify what they thought the particular issue was with reading achievement or with maths achievement. Most of the others were a little hazy about what was involved in this. Together they revisited the chapter on theory for improvement. The notion of having a theory seemed to be key to moving forward. They decided that at this point they needed some external expertise to help them work through this. After all, they could not evaluate their theory until they had one clearly articulated. This was a watershed for this school. Developing their theory guided what they would focus on in viewing practice and what data they would collect to try to explain the pattern of student achievement.

CASE STUDY 2: SCHOOL B

This school was a larger urban school, a full primary, with a diverse student population. There were two Māori-medium education classes. The school had a staff of 15 and a senior management team of three, including the principal. They had not been part of schooling improvement initiatives or other major professional learning projects that took a whole-school approach. Their decision to utilise the information in this book was something of a step into the unknown, but there was unanimous agreement that they wanted the best for their students and the idea of inquiry for improvement seemed to make a lot of sense. It was not some prescriptive programme and it did not involve endless meetings with other schools where little seemed to be accomplished (they had heard about this through colleagues elsewhere). Undertaking inquiry as a collective was something that would bind them together; increase cohesion.

The senior management team had met several times to discuss the ideas in recent publications (they had all had some fairly heavy holiday reading), including the two recent best evidence syntheses on professional learning and on leadership (Robinson et al., 2009), the publications that summarised learning from the Literacy Professional Development Project (Timperley & Parr, 2009), and *Ka Hikitia* (Ministry of Education, 2007). So, they felt they had some background to lead this inquiry undertaking, although they appreciated that they would still be feeling their way.

They had set aside a half day, then a number of after-school sessions in the several weeks following. In the half day they intended to discuss the more general inquiry cycle and continua from Chapter Two, and then divide into groups (across syndicate groupings), each taking two chapters. They allocated the chapters in a way that made sense to them. One group took Chapter Four, talking about professional learning, and also Chapter Eight, about professional discussions. Another took theory for improvement and also Māori-medium education, because they thought it would be useful to consider the valued outcomes notion in relation to both. The final group were to consider the classroom and data chapters. The plan was to spend two further after-school meetings in groups, then hold two report-back meetings. Below is the assembled template with the outcomes of the deliberations ready for the first report-back meeting. We briefly consider the initial reporting back from the discussions about what turned out to be a key area for this school.

SCHOOL B's PATTERN OF DECISIONS

Chapter Two (evidence and inquiry)

1. Identifying valued outcomes and student learning needs

BASIC	MIDDLE/MIXED	INTEGRATED

2. Identifying professional learning needs—leaders and teachers

BASIC	MIDDLE/MIXED	INTEGRATED

3. Engagement in professional learning to deepen knowledge and refine skills

BASIC	MIDDLE/MIXED	INTEGRATED

4. Engagement of students in new learning experiences

BASIC	MIDDLE/MIXED	INTEGRATED

Chapter Three (theory for improvement)

1. Understanding of likely interrelated causes of the problem

BASIC	MIDDLE/MIXED	INTEGRATED

2. Proposed evidence-based solutions to directly address the causes of the problem

BASIC	MIDDLE/MIXED	INTEGRATED

3. Interim and long-term targets against which progress can be judged

BASIC	MIDDLE/MIXED	INTEGRATED

4. Ways to monitor progress towards the targets

BASIC	MIDDLE/MIXED	INTEGRATED

Chapter Four (talking about change knowledge)

1. Identifying priorities

BASIC	MIDDLE/MIXED	INTEGRATED

2. Holding high expectations

BASIC	MIDDLE/MIXED	INTEGRATED

3. Communicating challenges

BASIC	MIDDLE/MIXED	INTEGRATED

4. Evaluating outcomes

BASIC	MIDDLE/MIXED	INTEGRATED

Chapter Five (Māori-medium education)

1. Identifying valued outcomes

BASIC	MIDDLE/MIXED	INTEGRATED

2. Leadership

BASIC	MIDDLE/MIXED	INTEGRATED

3. Professional development

BASIC	MIDDLE/MIXED	INTEGRATED

4. School development

BASIC	MIDDLE/MIXED	INTEGRATED

Chapter Six (classroom practice)

1. Selecting appropriate diagnostic measures to ascertain the pattern of development

BASIC	MIDDLE/MIXED	INTEGRATED

2. Students' understanding of their goals and learning

BASIC	MIDDLE/MIXED	INTEGRATED

3. Student engagement in self-assessment

BASIC	MIDDLE/MIXED	INTEGRATED

4. Use of information about student learning to evaluate practice

BASIC	MIDDLE/MIXED	INTEGRATED

Chapter Seven (ensuring quality data)

1. The purpose of collecting data and alignment with tools

BASIC	MIDDLE/MIXED	INTEGRATED

2. Rich data to allow explanation

BASIC	MIDDLE/MIXED	INTEGRATED

3. Trustworthiness

BASIC	MIDDLE/MIXED	INTEGRATED

4. Ensuring a fair and accurate assessment

BASIC	MIDDLE/MIXED	INTEGRATED

Chapter Eight (PCK and evidence-informed discussions)

1. Knowledge of subject content

BASIC	MIDDLE/MIXED	INTEGRATED

2. Knowledge of teaching subject to others

BASIC	MIDDLE/MIXED	INTEGRATED

The group that had considered how the school stood with respect to quality data and classroom practice negotiated that they lead off at the first report-back session. They felt that student achievement information underpinned everything, so this was why they should start the ball rolling. There was some dissension from the theory for improvement group, who said that after their deliberations they saw a lot of overlap, but they agreed to chip in where they felt it was needed.

The quality data/classroom group reported that although they had started by stating that the school did have goals and a purpose for collecting the data (they wanted half of their students to be performing at national expectations or above) and were lining up for middle-mixed, they had come to a realisation that this was a generalised goal that could be accomplished while a number of students still underachieved. Also, they were only too painfully aware that their decision to switch to a new assessment tool that was more fitted to their purpose to get information that would help in planning instruction had unintended consequences. It meant they could not judge progress by comparing the beginning and the end of the year just finished.

The information from the earlier tool, while telling them about their students' level of achievement relative to other students nationally, had not been that helpful in planning detailed professional development. They had gone ahead and undertaken professional development for guided reading, although, because they were not sure precisely what the detailed problems were with respect to student reading, they were not sure whether the professional development addressed them or not. It was true that guided reading, well done, was likely to be an effective practice. But could it be strengthened by a clear focus, geared to precise student need? And, given the lack of information about teacher knowledge and practice, it was not clear the extent to which the professional development was revision for some teachers, honing already sound practice, rather than providing impetus to a changed practice or element of practice that could have a clear effect on achievement. They had no data on classroom practice other than the confidential information from appraisals, and only two people were privy to each appraisal! Their professional learning sessions had not involved any critique or challenge to existing practice, and while it was assumed a teacher might change (perhaps if you got a "good idea"), the expectation of changed teacher practice was not "out there".

For this school, as the saying goes, the can of worms had been opened. But rather than bury it quickly, they were, like junior secondary science students, laying the contents out and dissecting them with great concentration and interest. The theory for improvement group did chip in (in fact they led the discussion at a number of points).

What eventuated was that the end-of-year, more diagnostic achievement data were discussed and a shared understanding of the problem in student achievement was arrived at. They planned to collect evidence on a number of candidate explanatory variables that, it was felt, would help explain the pattern of performance. Their theory for improvement was taking shape. Research was consulted to try to discover what solutions to their particular achievement problem had been successful elsewhere. There were plans to observe current practice to see the extent to which elements of these solutions from research already existed in practice.

And so the discussion went on. Some teachers went to collect children and then returned to continue the discussion. The principal left to go over to the board of trustees meeting and ask them to continue without him. The school was engaged in probably its first genuine professional learning community meeting. They were enjoying the sense of commonality and of autonomy, although they knew that there were a number of areas where they would need to seek expert help to learn from.

CASE STUDY 3: SCHOOL C: A SECONDARY SCHOOL EXAMPLE

School C is a decile 3 school with a roll of 1,500 students. The student population is very diverse, with the three main ethnic groups being Māori, Samoan and Pākehā. There are three main feeder intermediate schools and School C had worked hard to establish good relationships with them. The school has a number of professional development focuses, but the one on which they spent the most time was literacy across the curriculum. They particularly wanted teachers in departments other than English to understand the implications of students' asTTle reading results for their teaching.

The senior management team thought about how best to involve the staff in using the template, and decided that the best approach was for the principal, together with the deputy principal responsible for professional development, the head of English and other volunteers from the English department, to work on it. The reason for this composition was that the English department had taken to heart the mission of making every teacher a literacy teacher and so had become responsible for leading the professional development in this area. They decided to work through the book chapters systematically, while realising that they needed to make some adjustments to the descriptors for secondary schools. They began with Chapter Two and came up with the decisions below. They only got to Chapter Three, for reasons that are discussed below.

SCHOOL C's PATTERN OF DECISIONS

Chapter Two (evidence and inquiry)

1. Identifying valued outcomes and student learning needs

BASIC	MIDDLE/MIXED	INTEGRATED

2. Identifying professional learning needs—leaders and teachers

BASIC	MIDDLE/MIXED	INTEGRATED

3. Engagement in professional learning to deepen knowledge and refine skills

BASIC	MIDDLE/MIXED	INTEGRATED

4. Engagement of students in new learning experiences

BASIC	MIDDLE/MIXED	INTEGRATED

Chapter Three (theory for improvement)

1. Understanding of the likely interrelated causes of the problem

BASIC	MIDDLE/MIXED	INTEGRATED

2. Proposed evidence-based solutions to directly address the causes of the problem

BASIC	MIDDLE/MIXED	INTEGRATED

They began looking at the descriptors on the continuum related to identifying valued outcomes and student learning needs. They placed themselves at middle/ mixed because they had been routinely assessing students on asTTle reading for two years. They also used other subject-specific assessments. However, they suspected that the attention paid to the implications for teaching and learning from the asTTle assessment was variable across departments. In the English department, the teachers in the group thought they were approaching integrated, but the "whole school community" descriptor meant they did not meet the requirements of this descriptor as a school.

On the next dimension, about identifying professional learning needs, they agreed that they fitted the middle/mixed description. They had identified the need for professional development in literacy across the curriculum from the students' asTTle reading results, and this had been discussed at length by all the teachers in the school-based professional development sessions. The head of English had attended a meeting to raise awareness of the importance of addressing literacy across the curriculum if the lower achieving students were to meet the reading requirements of external examinations in NCEA. The senior management team had reorganised the timetable to have a professional development session first thing every Wednesday morning. The rotating focus for these sessions gave more time to literacy than any other topic. The professional development had mainly involved giving teachers from other departments ideas about literacy-related activities they could use during their lessons. The technology department particularly liked the vocabulary-building activities they could use during the inevitable down time that occurred in some lessons.

They disagreed about where they fitted on the dimension related to engagement in professional learning to deepen knowledge and refine skills. The professional development was provided primarily by the head of English and other members of the English department, so they were at the integrated level on that aspect of the dimension. They were not reliant on external expertise. But when they thought about the descriptors related to teacher participation, it seemed they were at a more basic level. Although everyone was required to attend the Wednesday morning sessions, it was obvious that real engagement was variable, both across and within departments. The technology department and some teachers from more literacy-oriented subjects appeared to show greater interest than others, and a history teacher had even brought along a text to analyse the reading demands and what would be needed to scaffold the students to meet them.

The fourth dimension—engagement of students in new experiences—was clearly at a basic level. Variability in implementation was both an expected and accepted feature of secondary schools. No-one had any real idea of the extent to which any changes had occurred in classrooms because observations of practice occurred only in conjunction with appraisal, and the criteria used in the observations depended on the department head.

When they got to Chapter Three, on theories for improvement, the group struggled a bit with the idea of what a theory for improvement really was and why it mattered. It was obvious that for student achievement to improve in NCEA, all Years 9 and 10 teachers needed to be literacy teachers (and probably in Year 11 as well). They had moved way beyond thinking that the cause of the problem lay in the homes the students came from or the quality of teaching in the primary and intermediate schools. They had taken the decision to do something themselves about the literacy problems experienced by many of their students and were not looking to others to fix the problem for them. What was the point of looking for a cause? It was the solution that mattered.

They needed to read the descriptors through to the integrated level, and those related to the proposed solutions, to realise that this idea of cause applied to unpacking what it was that students could do or not do in reading subject-specific material and whether there was shared agreement about this across the different departments. They realised that the point of identifying the cause was that the solution needs to relate to an analysis of the cause. After playing with this idea for some time, they also realised that one of their problems was that they had become so passionate about getting every teacher to be a teacher of literacy that they had not undertaken an analysis of the specialised literacy demands needed in each curriculum area. As they talked the issue through it became obvious that it was deeper than knowing the technical vocabulary of science or how to develop an argument in history. Without having unpacked the literacy demands for each subject area in greater detail, they realised why the teachers could talk about generic causes only (e.g., "Our asTTle marks are low because the kids can't handle the text") with similarly generic solutions (e.g., "Teach subject-specific vocabulary"). As English teachers, they also realised they could not unpack detailed causes and solutions without involving staff with specialist knowledge in their area of the curriculum.

Going further through the continua in the different chapters did not seem to be a particularly productive idea until they sorted out this problem, although a quick glance at Chapter Four, about change talk, made them realise they had inadvertently avoided any talk of change. They wanted to make the introduction of literacy across the curriculum seem more seamless, and did not want to scare staff by talking about the extent of change they believed was needed. However, they decided to shelve really thinking about how to do this until they had done the analysis of the literacy demands across the different curriculum areas.

They came back to the more immediate problem of how to involve other departments in unpacking the literacy demands of their subject areas. They suspected that if they worked with the heads of departments, they may get more buy-in. The head of English also remembered that at the earlier meeting she had attended, about the importance of literacy across the curriculum, someone mentioned that one of the advisory services had undertaken an analysis along these lines. She thought that would be a good starting point. The strategy they settled on was to contact their local advisory service and find out if such an analysis existed. If it did exist, then they would take it to each department head to work through the analysis together and how they could share responsibility for working with the teachers. They figured that working in subject departments with shared responsibility for professional development was much more likely to get buy-in than the English department being seen as the experts. This "expert" label had left them feeling they all had the responsibility for getting others sufficiently motivated to see what was really involved, and for providing all the resources.

Afterword

All of the contributors to this book, through their experience in school improvement, school change and other related professional learning projects, both within New Zealand and internationally, know that it *is* possible to raise achievement for *all* students. They would, however, be the first to hasten to add that it is not straightforward or gained without considerable effort by all those involved. The authors are all committed to the idea of the power of inquiry and evidence to bring about change and improvement. That standards and similar benchmarks are used in ways that enhance learning, melding with core business rather than detracting from it, is something they are keen to work on with partners to ensure it happens. We all want the best for our New Zealand students (and students everywhere). As a group, we hope this book has provided something of use to you and wish you well in your inquiry and endeavours.

References

Ministry of Education. (2007). *Ka hikitia—Managing for success: The draft Māori Education Strategy 2008–2012*. Wellington: Author.

Robinson, V., Hōhepa, M., & Lloyd, C. (2009). *School leadership and student outcomes: Identifying what works and why: Best evidence synthesis iteration*. Wellington: Ministry of Education.

Coaching Leadership:
Building educational leadership capacity through coaching partnerships
Jan Robertson

Coaching Leadership is about building leadership capacity in individuals, and in institutions, through enhancing professional relationships. It is based on the importance of maximising potential, and harnessing the ongoing commitment and energy needed to meet personal and professional goals. Based on over a decade of research and development, nationally and internationally, *Coaching Leadership* brings you the empirical evidence, the principles, and the skills, to be able to develop your own leadership and that of others you work with.

This book:

Challenges you to critically reflect on your leadership and professional relationships;

Offers practical activities and exercises;

Describes leadership coaching based on reciprocal processes;

Seeks to connect theory and practice;

Provides a basis for workshop activities in coaching, appraisal, and mentoring.

This book comes highly recommended to those professionals committed to lifelong, experiential learning and reflective practice.

An essential addition to the professional development programme.

"Jan Robertson's splendid book not only advocates articulately for the necessity of leadership coaching, but sets out practically what good coaching can, and should, look like." Andy Hargreaves, Boston College.

NZCER Press 2005   ISBN 978-1-877398-02-5   Price: $39.95

For a full list of publications from NZCER Press go to:
www.nzcer.org.nz/nzcerpress

NZCER PRESS

Lightning Source UK Ltd.
Milton Keynes UK
UKOW02f2043030114

223971UK00009B/474/P

9 781877 398605